TOP OF THE LINE

FISHING COLLECTIBLES

Donna Tonelli

77 Lower Valley Road, Atglen, PA 19310

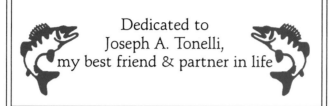

Dedicated to
Joseph A. Tonelli,
my best friend & partner in life

Printed in China
ISBN: 0-7643-0209-4
Book Design By Audrey L. Whiteside

Library of Congress Cataloging-in-Publication Data

Tonelli, Donna.
    Top of the line fishing collectibles/Donna Tonelli.
        p.   cm.
    Includes bibliographical references (p.   ) and index.
    ISBN 0-7643-0209-4
    1. Fishing--Equipment and supplies--Collectibles--
United States--Catalogs. I. Title.
SH453.T66   1997
688.7'91'0973075--dc21   96-49087
                                       CIP

Published by Schiffer Publishing, Ltd.
77 Lower Valley Road
Atglen, PA 19310
Phone: (610) 593-1777
Fax: (610) 593-2002
E-mail: schifferbk@aol.com
Please write for a free catalog.
This book may be purchased from the publisher.
Please include $2.95 for shipping.
Try your bookstore first.

We are interested in hearing from authors
with book ideas on related subjects.

Contents

ACKNOWLEDGMENTS

Before I thank the people who helped me complete this text, I want to give a special acknowledgment to the folks of northern Minnesota. Had they not been as open and warm as they were, Joe and I would have never learned to love the north woods as we do, and we certainly wouldn't have been able to build our fishing paraphernalia collection. Decoy carvers like Chet Sawyer, Chuck Hall, and the families and friends of men like them, shared their living histories and helped us understand the sport of spearing, what it meant to their everyday lives, and how they created their art. When we first started to collect fishing tackle and decoys, many of these people found items for us. We have spent many hours at flea markets, estate sales and visiting with them. These are special people and I am proud to call them friends.

Ron Adamson, White Bear Lake
Orvile Anderson, Grand Rapids
Jim and Diane Cook, Minneapolis
John Cook, Remer
Rick & Jay Davis, Deer River
"Digger"
Jerome & Bonnie Erickson, Nissawa
John Goplerud, Park Rapids
Bill & Mary Green, LaPrairie
Dan Handeland, Cushing
Ollie & Stella Oslon, Wadena
Dave Perkins, Duluth
John Plank, Bovey
Will Reiner, Balsam Lake
Jim & Mary Richards, Calloway
Bob & Ruthie Shoop, Longville
Louis and Maridee Smilich, Deerwood
Stan, the Man

Anyone who has taken on a project like this needs to know he can depend on other collectors to fill the gaps. I have been fortunate that several knowledgeable people stepped forward to help me. First and foremost was my husband, Joe who patiently let me 'pick his brain' and critiqued every step of this project so I wouldn't forget anything important. Others who provided photography and information are:

Frank Baron
Dan Basore
John Banholzer
John and Tina Delph
Alan and Elaine Haid
Bud Hendrickson
Ron Holloway
David Fisher
LuAnn Frobes
Gregg and Kay Gruthie
Gene and Linda Kangas
Art Kimball
Jim McCleery
Ben Meyers
Pete Meyers
Heidi Price
George Raden
John Shoffner
NOTE: Unless otherwise identified all illustrations are from the collection of Joseph A. and Donna Tonelli.

4

INTRODUCTION

I have been collecting all of my married life with my husband, Joe. We were fortunate to live in the heart of the finest waterfowling in the midwest. Within minutes of our home, the greatest Illinois River decoy carvers produced and sold their hunting decoys, boats and calls. We have amassed a fine collection and developed many strong friendships based on the common bond of sporting collectibles.

During the late 1970s, Joe was hired to manage a wildlife refuge in northern Minnesota, so we spent our summers and autumns there. We tried to pick up duck decoys like we had in Illinois, but found that Minnesota carvers usually made crude black blocks or nondescript silhouettes for waterfowling. What we did discover were fish decoys and old fishing tackle. Used to lure large predator fish while ice fishing with a spear, Minnesota fish decoys have all the style and form that their waterfowling de-

coys lacked. And northern Minnesota was 'virgin territory'. Few people had recognized the collecting potential of the fish decoys or old baits. It was collecting deja vu for us. Instead of finding duck decoys in boat houses and barns, we were looking for dark houses in back yards; digging through tackle boxes and old coffee cans in garages. With no documentation and only our experience dealing with old hunting decoys to help us, we bought anything that looked good, kept what we felt was the best, and sold off the extras to pay for our growing collection of old fishing tackle and related folk art.

Fishing paraphernalia from all parts of the midwest has become a major part of our antique collection. As we visited with old fish decoy makers, I started to gather oral histories and one thing became apparent: these men were as colorful and interesting as their carvings. They produced tackle that was functional and beautiful. Most were rugged

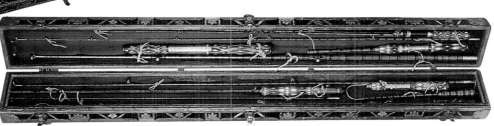

The quality of the workmanship used to produce this magnificent fishing rod set is clear evidence that although many of the men who created fishing collectibles were untrained, they were by no means unskilled. Raymond Thompson (1887-1966) was not considered successful by most of his contemporaries in Park Rapids, Minnesota. He worked as a barber, did odd jobs and often purposely got himself arrested for poaching so he could spend the coldest winter months in the county jail rent free. It is believed he made this rod set while he was in the county jail, c.1930. $20,000-25,000.

outdoorsmen yet when simple equipment would do, they took pride in having everyday items like bait boxes and jigging sticks that were decorated. Simple bamboo rods with cork handles were wrapped with colored silk line and inlaid with bits of ivory; proof that common untrained men are often excellent artisans. Many of these men earned a living selling their baits and decoys to local sportsmen and visiting fishermen in hardware and sporting goods stores. Still others went on to establish tackle companies. Skills from totally unrelated trades were incorporated to develop new and improved tools for the sports of angling and ice fishing. Watchmakers became reel manufacturers. Metal workers produced fine hollow copper fish decoys. This is why fishing paraphernalia is becoming recognized as a major form of American collectibles.

In this book, I want to share some of the folklore I have learned and to present the reader with an overview of what collecting fishing paraphernalia has to offer the collector. Since collecting fishing paraphernalia is a relatively new field, evaluations are usually based on personal taste and a general feel for an item. Prices are frankly very subjective and vary from dealer to dealer.

Regional collectors appraise local collectibles accordingly. Values given in the book reflect the subjective appraisals of the individual collectors and dealers. While I respect their judgments, these prices must be considered simply as guidelines.

As with most collectibles, one must be careful to deal with reputable dealers who will stand behind their sales. As author of this text, I guarantee that all the items shown are authentic antique fishing collectibles. There are artisans who are producing fish decoys, plaques, and lures in an attempt to cash in on the old fishing tackle craze. In most cases anyone who takes the time to study known reproductions can easily learn to distinguish the real thing. I recommend that those interested in learning more about collecting fishing collectibles refer to the bibliography for a listing of related readings and collector organizations that specialize in sporting collectibles. They can provide invaluable information, sources, and good fellowship.

6

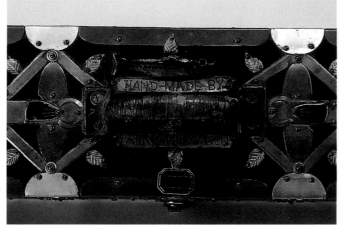

Top detail.

Thompson designed this carrying case by drawing upon his experience as a coffin maker, one of his many odd jobs. The inside is tucked with purple fabric and the entire footed case is embellished with fine filigree leaves and metal inlays.

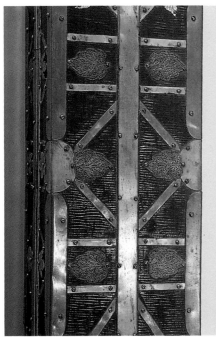

Thompson also incorporated his decoy carving skills by adding small wooden trout under the handle and inside the carrying case.

Top detail.

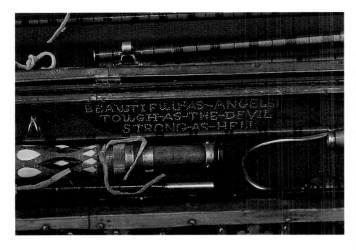

This is the only known set of "Blue Water Specials" which Thompson produced. Brass tags mounted inside the case declare: "Dexterous Rods - Deluxe Models - Superb Supreme", "Craftsmanship Materials Guaranteed", "Beautiful as Angels - Tough As The Devil - Strong as Hell". Proud claims From "Craftsman- Ray Thompson".

Handles.

Thompson made a simple bamboo rod pattern when he created his "Blue Water Specials" which included a double tipped fly rod, a light-weight panfish rod, a bass rod and a heavy duty musky rod. Then he wrapped the entire length of each rod with fine silk thread and lacquered the rod with several coats of varnish. The cork handles were shaped and embellished with tiny bits of ivory.

The Thompson "Blue Water" set was complete with miscellaneous fishing tools, a gaff, a hookless practice casting plug and a hook remover. Each of these tools were also wrapped with silk thread and varnished.

Chapter 1
Fish Decoys

Introduction

In a time when the simple beauty of the everyday products of early American life are being appreciated more and more, the fish decoy is becoming part of the ever growing list of recognized folk art forms. The basic concept behind the success of a fish decoy was that big fish eat little fish. A small weighted fish decoy would be lowered through a hole cut into the frozen surface of a lake. Here it would be jigged to recreate the actions of a live fish, hopefully attracting a large prey fish within striking range of the fisherman's spear. A darkhouse or tent would be placed over the hole to seal out all outside light. The first glance through the hole reveals only translucent green water, but as one's eyes adjust to the surrounding darkness, details are illuminated by the light that filters through the ice. Eel grass and feathery milfoil slowly weave amidst the rocks and shells on the lake bottom. An experienced fishermen would often drop something white, like potato peelings, egg shells or dried beans to the bottom to create a white backdrop for his decoy and any action that occur below his hole.

The fish reacted to the decoy differently. Some would slowly swim beneath the decoy, often laying almost motionless for awhile before it would cautiously approach the decoy. Others would attack so swiftly that the fisherman had little chance of striking it with

The essence of spear fishing is captured here by Fred Lexow, Balsam Lake, Minnesota in his colored pen and ink drawing depicting a northern responding to a Lexow decoy. A multitude of wavy lines merge like a French Impressionist painting, yet Lexow had no professional training, 16"x 20", c.1940. $1000-1500.

his spear. The fisherman would rest the spearhead on the edge of the ice hole, because he may have to wait for hours for a single strike. When a fish was sighted, he would gently edge his spearhead into the water to prevent a large splash that might spook his prey when his spear was casted. The long handle of the weighted spear would usually be attached to a strong rope that was tied to a heavy object or a beam in the darkhouse because a large prey fish weighing thirty pounds or more could pull a man off balance. The tines of the spear were razor sharp and barbed to hold the fish fast if the fisherman needed to wait for the fish to tire before it could be retrieved.

A fish decoy needed to perform certain functions. Most essential was that it would sink quickly into the water. Since the most common decoy material was wood, extra weight was needed. Most decoy makers gouged a cavity into the underbelly of their decoy. Molten lead was poured into this cavity. To be practical, a decoy had to be waterproof. Some makers fashioned their decoy out of metal, molding it or simply cutting out a silhouette. Later manufacturers molded plastic decoys. The most collectible decoys are wooden. A variety of native woods were used by carvers: white cedar, pines and redwood. To seal the wooden decoys coats of waterproof paint were applied.

The determining function of a decoy was to attract fish. The decoy relied on appearance and movement to alert its prey. To swim correctly the decoy needed added fins to stabilize its movement. One or two metal fins were set perpendicularly on each side of the body. Anal and dorsal fins were added for looks. The tail also determined the type of motion the decoy would make. A curve would be carved into the decoy body or a flexible metal tail would be added that could be bent to change the decoy's action. When suspended from a jigging stick, a decoy could be made to slowly circle, do a "figure 8", or imitate an injured fish with a simple change in the movement of the angler's wrist. Motion and how a decoy relates to the water may be the least recognized facet of the fish decoy.

The art of the decoy was in how the craftsmen interpreted what looked inviting to the fish. Most makers created a variety of decoys knowing that water conditions altered fish behavior. A single ice fisherman's box could hold several styles of decoys: realistic fish, abstract designs, natural wood finishes, solid color fish, and metal decoys. As in all art forms, the makers developed their individual styles that could be seen in their work. The following text will attempt to identify the works of some of the men who are being recognized as newly discovered folk artists. Not all these carvers have been identified yet their work displays such strong style that it needs no name to be appreciated.

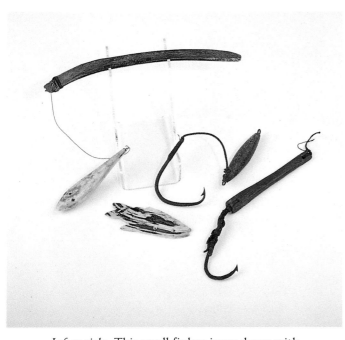

10

Left to right: This small finless ivory decoy with embedded metal eyes is typical of the prehistoric fishing decoy. It is suspended from its original curved bone jigging stick. Cut from a large fresh water mussel shell, this silhouette fish has holes where bits of thread or feathers once hung. Found near the LaCrosse, Wisconsin area, it is believed to predate the settlement by European settlers. Large hand held iron hooks like these were used by early Native Americans to catch fresh water fish. *Courtesy private collection.*

Trio of anonymous Inuit prehistoric fish decoys, Norton Era, c.500 BC, carved ivory or bone, 3"- 5", found during an archaeological excavation near Sishmaret, Alaska. $200-300 each. *Photo by Gene Kangas. Courtesy of Gene and Linda Kangas.*

Today's collectors would like to believe that fish decoys originated in the western hemisphere, in North America particularly. While there is no evidence that fish decoying was practiced in Europe, archaeologists have found stones chipped into fish shapes in the Neolithic sites of the Pribaikal region in southeast Siberia leading them to assume that they were the first fish decoys which would have been used in north central Asia 3000 to 7000 years ago. The use of fish decoys is documented throughout much of northern Asia in the Asia Pacific Northeast from northern Japan northward, around the Bering Straits, and elsewhere in the northeastern regions of the continent by such groups as the Ainu, Koryak and Samoyer.[1] Ancient Japanese silk paintings depict the Ainu people spearing through the ice under a semi-conical mat darkhouse. Then, as in modern times, spearing fish through the ice provided a reliable food source during the difficult winter season. As primitive man migrated across the Bering Strait into North America, he continued to rely on spear fishing during the harshest season of the year for his major source of food. Like the modern fish decoy makers, early nomadic tribesmen used the natural resources around them to craft their decoys. The Eskimo tribes from Alaska to Quebec and Labrador used fish decoys that were usually simple bone or ivory oblong shapes yet examples have been found that display fine craftsmanship and beautiful detailing. Bits of leather or feathers were sometimes added as fins. Usually a single hole was bored through the decoy's dorsal area where sinew could be drawn through allowing the fisherman to suspend the decoy into the water and work it to attract his prey. Most of the Arctic and subarctic tribes fashioned decoys out of ivory and bone, although a very few examples of wooden decoys have been excavated. .

Shell fish decoys (circa 1300) found in Fulton County, Illinois represent the southern most archaeological fish decoy finds.[2] Ancient decoys made from mussel shells were used throughout the Great Lakes region. The French explorer, Antoine Denis Raudot described the hunting and fishing techniques of the "savages of the North" in a letter he wrote in 1709 saying; "to attract the fish they use a small fish of porcelain which they play in the water attached to the end of a stick".[3] According to the editor of *Jesuit Relations and Allied Documents*, Ruben G. Thwaits, porcelain is "simply the French-Canadian term for shell, glass or porcelain beads used as money and ornaments by the Indians". More than forty such decoys have been recorded in archaeological sites from Nebraska to Saint Ste. Marie and from Southern Illinois to Minnesota. These carvings were sometimes detailed with eyes, gills, mouths and scales by native craftsmen. Often holes were made for leather fins. Earliest examples of shell fish date from 1000 or 1100 AD.

By the 1700s, the use of fish decoys was being practiced by most Indian tribes of the Great Lakes region including Minnesota, New York, Michigan, and Wisconsin. Eyewitness accounts by early settlers and traders describe various tribes, especially the Ojibwa, using fish decoys in conjunction with a dark hut made of branches and skins or blankets and *leisters*, i.e. fish spears. By this time most Native American fish decoys were fashion out of native woods. Prior to the availability of lead from the fur traders, Indians weighted their decoys with stones which were tied into a body cavity. A small pack thread was tied around the body to suspend it. Bits of yarn, leather, or feather embellishments may have been added to the body. Metal tails often complemented metal fins. Charring was a common method of decorating fish decoys although there are many examples of painted Indian fish. Details like gills, eyes, mouth, and possibly cross-hatchings were burned into the wood using a hot brad. Thicker charred vertical strips often denoted darker shadings of a fish's natural coloration. Unfortunately many collectors tend to label any decoy that is left unpainted with wood-burned decorations as Indian-made. This does the Native American carver a great injustice. Painted Native American decoys may have creative abstract patterns in bright colors or muted realistic colored stains

Production of fish decoys by Native Americans spans centuries from the earliest mussel shell and bone decoys to the modern

11

John "Waazhashk" Snow, Lac du Flambeau Reservation, Wisconsin, recognized nationally as a fish decoy carver, is part a growing revival of Native American culture and crafts. These early examples of his decoys retain a graceful flowing style and bold expression that is not seen in his later more commercial work, c.1950. *Photo by Alan D. Subera. Courtesy of Gregg and Kay Guthrie.*

day resurgence of the art by men like John Snow, Lac du Flambeau reservation, Wisconsin. John Snow was featured by the Smithsonian Institute as a Native American artisan. Although his work has taken on a slightly commercial quality which overshadows his earlier graceful flowing style and bold free manner of expressing the relationship between the fish and fisherman, it is an excellent example of the quality of Indian fish decoys. Even though few individual makers have been identified, their work is strongly personal and can be classified by reservations. There are no known commercial fish decoy makers among the Native American tribesmen. Most Indian carvers made up decoys as they needed them and often discarded them at the end of the season. Even today they find it hard to understand why anyone would "collect" fish decoys and keep them in their homes.

Although the earliest explorers and trappers most likely observed the Native Indian methods of winter fishing, latter settlers probably experimented with fish decoys after reading about them in published accounts by early traders and explorers. These accounts served

as popular advertisements to attract new settlers for the Americas. The immigrants adapted their woodworking techniques and painting skills to develop a polychromed wooden decoy. Each maker drew upon his own experiences to create his own interpretation of the fish, thus the decoys became expressions of the fisherman's prey — a functioning art form.

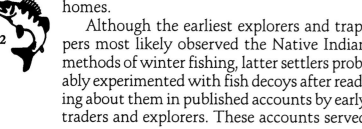

John "Waazhashk" Snow, Lac du Flambeau Reservation, Wisconsin, with contemporary frog decoy, c.1990. *Courtesy of private collection.*

Unlike the nomadic natives of this new land, the immigrants carved out homesteads and settled into one place, picking sites that had fresh water and wild game nearby. As they cleared the land and developed agricultural sources, the first settlers had to rely upon the land to provide their food supply. This influenced the development of the fish decoy because the makers had the time to improve their product. Since they did not move with the seasons, equipment from the previous year was stored rather than discarded. Their decoys were not quickly made as they were needed, but worked on during slow times as a leisure activity. Eyes of glass, beads, spent bullets, or other ingenious materials were added to the fish form. Gills and mouth were carved into the body while dorsal and anal fins were added for realism. Side fins were mounted perpendicular to the body to stabilize the decoy movement in the water. A curved body or metal tail was used to vary the decoy's movements as in was drawn towards the surface to enhance its luring powers. All these features were assimilated with the simple fish decoy the Indians' shared with the new inhabitants of their lands.

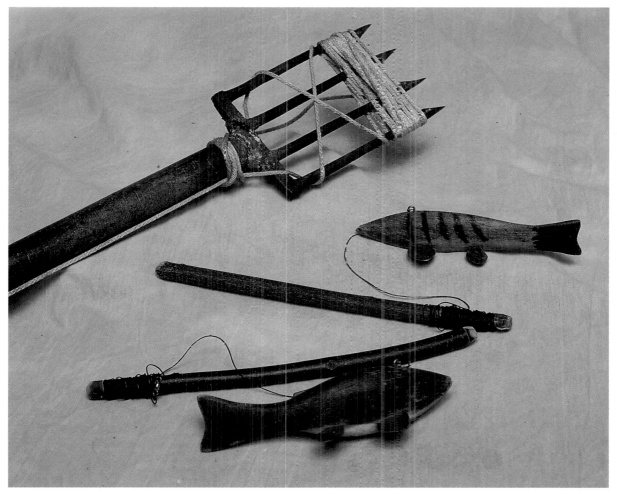

Augie Allen, Lac du Flambeau Reservation, carries on the decoy carving tradition started by his father Ross Allen Sr. These early examples of his personal decoys are shown with his fishing spear, c.1960. *Photo by Alan D. Subera. Courtesy of Gregg and Kay Guthrie.*

13

By the 1880s, the fish decoy was used throughout the northern Great Lakes states of Michigan, New York, Wisconsin, and Minnesota. Small towns of little wooden shanties sprung up on the frozen lakes each winter as the fish were harvested for personal use and the market. These darkhouses, too, were stored and reused each season. The darkhouse was a simple wooden building with no windows usually just large enough for one man to sit comfortably over a hole cut into the floor. Small stoves were used to keep warm. Sometimes there was even room for a small cot allowing a fisherman to stay on the ice for days. Runners were affixed to the darkhouses enabling one man to pull the shanty to his favorite fishing spot. It became customary for the local fish monger to drive out through the ice fishing shanty towns with his wagon purchasing fish. Before legal restrictions any fish was fair game for the ice fisherman. The fish would be piled on the ice outside of the shanties, "freshly frozen" for the market, usually selling for a few pennies per pound — bass, perch, crappie, sunfish, northern pike, sturgeon, and muskellunge.

It is not surprising that the spear fisherman became the outcast of the growing fraternity of sports fishermen. Governmental game regulations were enacted which limited this form of fishing to protect the game fish. Today only northern pike and sturgeon are allowed to be speared under strict regulations. Yet the fish decoys and other spearing equipment, often decorated by local craftsmen, remain as a testimony to another time that has passed. These intriguing bits of folk art were made by men who live in the northern lake lands. With no markets or extra cash nearby, their art was made with limited resources — local woods, used tins, cheap glass beads, hardware store paints. Hardly the makings of great art, yet the subtlety of their work captures one's eye.

Some decoy makers developed small cottage industries. Their markets included tourists, local hardware stores, and bait shops. When commercial tackle companies came into existence, they often included fish decoys in their product lines. These decoys were machined and hand finished on a simple production line that utilized air-compressed

Art Lyons carved fish decoys to use when he guided on Lake Winnibigoshish, Leech Lake Reservation, Minnesota, c.1940. *Courtesy of private collection.*

14

Native American fish decoys are not always left in a natural finish and wood burned. This set of spearing decoys, found on the Red lake Reservation, north of Bemidji, Minnesota, exemplify the charm and artistry found in Native American crafts. The large fish is bi-colored, orange on one side, green on the other. The large frog has movable legs and red jeweled eyes, c.1920. $4,000-5,000 set.

painting techniques and piece assembly with uniform metal hardware. Thus the modern day fish decoy ranges from simple wooden Indian decoys with charred detailing to fanciful fish by local fishermen and the highly stylized decoy assembled by the tackle companies. Each has its own appeal.

The following are various examples of spear fishing decoys catagorized by several classes or "schools" of decoys. As a part of these schools, individual decoys may share several identifying traits, i.e. species, style, type of constructing material, or possibly where they were made.

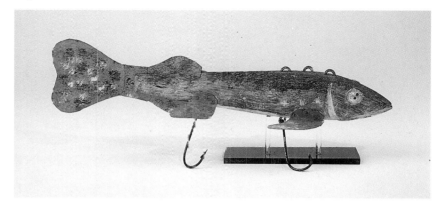

Found in Marquehe, Michigan, this Native American decoy is considered a "cheater" because the large trailing hooks often snagged a striking fish. Note the interesting tail configuration, c.1950. *Courtesy of private collection.*

LAKE CHAUTAUQUA DECOYS

Beautiful Lake Chautauqua, located in the southwestern corner of New York state, was a center for commercial winter fishing during the late 1800s. Local newspapers regularly reported the spear fishermen's success in harvesting thousands of muskellunge from the waters of the lake. When the numbers of muskellunge dropped dramatically during the early 1900s, reports lamented; "Remember the tons of fish ...brought to this city each spearing day, by the wheelbarreful, conditions certainly have changed." Starting as early as 1856, conservationists tried to regulate the spear fishing on the lake, but it wasn't until 1905 that the governor signed the final mandate that would abolish spear fishing in New York completely. This information leads most collectors to believe that the Lake Chautauqua school of carving represents the earliest non-native examples of fish decoys and are some of the most desirable of the collectible fish decoys.

Lake Chautauqua fish decoys have several strong characteristics that are consistent with most decoys from this area. The unique use of leather to form a tail is almost a must for the collector. A thick slab of leather was notched and tapered to fit into a slit at the end of the slender, usually straight, wooden decoy body. Most Chautauqua fish are painted in subtle natural colors to represent specific species usually chub, bass, minnow, muskellunge, perch, northern pickerel, salmon, trout, sunfish, shiner, sucker, and walleye. Details like carved mouths and gills are common as are tack eyes. These fish rarely measure more than five to eight inches. As a rule, the tie line was drawn through a small hole drilled directly through the dorsal area of the decoy or attached to a single wire loop embedded into the decoy.

Since most Lake Chautauqua decoys were made near or before the turn of the century few of the individual makers have been identified. This does not, however, detract from the value of New York fish decoys due to their quality, rarity, and age.

Early 19th century spear fishermen pull their darkhouses onto the frozen Lake Chautauqua located in the southwestern corner of New York state. Like many northern lakes, Lake Chautauqua became a temporary home for countless spear fishermen during the winter months. *Photo by George Norton, 1899. Courtesy of Linda and Gene Kangas.*

16

Top right: Classic later style trout by Harry A. Seymour, Bemus, New York, c.1870. Seymour is considered the most prolific and desirable of the Lake Chautauqua fish decoys. $4000-5000. *Center:* Unknown maker, Lake Chautauqua, atypical metal tail, tack eyes, original jigging stick. c.1880. $3000-4000. *Bottom:* Unknown maker, Lake Chautauqua, painted tack eyes, bored tie line hole, copper fins, leather tail, and exceptional paint pattern. Distinctive anal and dorsal fins suggest this may be a Seymour decoy. Brown trout, c.1870. $4000-5000.

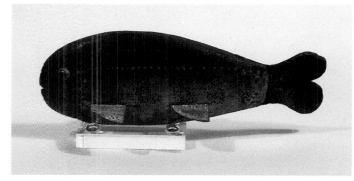

Sunfish, leather tail, copper tack eyes, Seymour or Cheney family, c.1870. $4000-5000. *Photo by Gene Kangas. Courtesy of Gene and Linda Kangas.*

17

The darkhouse provided protection from the elements and created the lightless environment needed to see clearly into the waters below the fishing hole as the fisherman worked his decoy attracting the large predator fish within striking range of his spear. Evergreen boughs provided extra insulation from the freezing ice and shut out sunlight that might filter through the surrounding ice. *Photo by George Norton, 1899. Courtesy of Linda and Gene Kangas.*

Fish decoys were used to attract large fish. A prize catch could easily exceed fifty pounds. This sturgeon caught by Rose Egnoski in Lake Winnebago, Wisconsin is as big as her, c.1950. A rope often tied the spear to a cinder block or the darkhouse rafters to hold the fish until it tired enough to be drawn out of the water.
Courtesy of Rose Egnoski.

ANGLING LICENSE

Angling License: 50c per individ- for family (the term "family" is the immediate family, i. e., husband or guardian). Non-resident angling .00, 16 years of age and over.

on-resident may ship to himself at station, 24 pounds of game fish in gate, or one fish weighing over that

LIMITS, FISH

	Per Day	In Possession
Pike (or Saugers)	8	16
or G. N. Pike)	10	16
ellow)	20	
	No limit, subject to restrictions by Director.	
ze	2	
ck, striped, yellow, rey)		25
lake trout)	6	25
	15	25 trout

it and Sal fish, red fish, suc whitefi lheads ck bass, t named e nore of inds or g limits, in exceeding a kind of g

1935 OPEN AND CLOSE FISHING S

WALL-EYED PIKE, SAND PIKE (or SAUG-ERS), PICKEREL, GREAT NORTHERN PIKE, YELLOW PERCH, May 15 to March 1. MUSKEL-LUNGE, May 15 to Feb. 1.
CRAPPIES: May 29 to Feb. 1, Southern Zone. June 21 to Feb. 1, Northern Zone.
BASS: (Striped, grey, yellow, black, silver, rock) May 29 to Dec. 1, Southern Zone; June 21 to Dec. 1, Northern Zone.
SUNFISH: May 29 to Dec. 1, Southern Zone; June 21 to Dec. 1, Northern Zone (except Goodhue County: May 29 to Feb. 1).
BULLHEADS, CATFISH, GARFISH, WHITE-FISH (not less than 16 inches), CARP, DOGFISH, REDHORSE, SHEEPSHEAD, SUCKERS, EEL-POUT, BUFFALO: All year, by angling, any time except March and April.
TROUT (any variety except lake trout): May 1 to Sept. 1. Except Lake, St. Louis, Itasca, Koochi-ching, Carlton, and Cook counties: May 15 to Sept. 1.
LAKE TROUT and SALMON: Nov. 15 to Sept. 15.
Netting WHITEFISH, TULLI use only—not for Dec. 25

SALE OF FISH PROHIBITED

Game fish of any variety taken under angling license, may not be bought or sold at any time.

FISH HOUSES

All the fish named under "Spearing Fish" also tullibees, may be taken by spearing or angling through the ice from a fish house or shelter and dark houses from December 1 to March 1, both dates inclusive. Only Carp so taken may be sold. Only one fish house may be used by one person. License $1.00; must be carried by person fishing and number marked on exterior of house. Regular fishing license also required.

SPEARING FISH

*BY THE GOVERNOR'S ORDER SPEARING IS PROHIBITED UNTIL MAY 14th, INC., IN THE SOUTHERN FISHING ZONE AND MAY 19th, INC., IN THE NORTHERN FISHING ZONE.

*Great Northern Pike, Pickerel, in the daytime in lakes and streams, except March 2 to May 14, both dates inclusive.

*Carp, dogfish, buffalofish, redhorse, sheepshead, suckers, eelpout, garfish (whitefish, not less than 16 inches), all year in lakes and streams in day time, subject to the limitation that these fish may be speared through the ice only from Dec. 1st to March 1st. Catfish and bullheads may be speared through the ice from Dec. 1st to March 1st.

*The use of artificial lights as an aid in spearing is permitted IN STREAMS ONLY in Zone 1, which includes the following counties: From April 15 to June 15, dates inclusive.

Blue Earth	Freeborn	Lincoln	Olmsted	Scott
Brown	Faribault	Martin	Pipestone	Sibley
Carver	Goodhue	Murray	Rock	Watonwan
Cottonwood	Houston	Mower	Rice	Waseca
Dakota	Jackson	McLeod	Redwood	Winona
Dodge	LeSueur	Nobles	Renville	Wabasha
Fillmore	Lyon	Nicollet	Steele	Yellow Medicine

Zone 2, which includes the following counties: From May 1st to June 15th, dates inclusive.

Aitkin	Crow Wing	Kandiyohi	Ottertail	Traverse
Anoka	Chisago	Kanabec	Pope	Todd
Benton	Chippewa	Lac Qui Parle	Pine	Washington
Becker	Douglas	Mahnomen	Ramsey	Wilkin
Big Stone	Grant	Meeker	Swift	Wadena
Cass	Hennepin	Mille Lacs	Stevens	Wright
Clay	Hubbard	Morrison	Stearns	
Carlton	Isanti	Norman	Sherburne	

The use of artificial lights as an aid in spearing is not permitted in Zone 3, which includes the following counties:

Beltrami	Itasca	Lake	Pennington	Roseau
Cook	Kittson	Lake of the Woods	Polk	St. Louis
Clearwater	Koochiching	Marshall	Red Lake	

These counties are subject to the provisions of Mason's Minnesota Statutes of 1927, Section 5499, as amended by Laws 1929, Chapter 417, which is to the effect that it shall be unlawful to take fish of any kind in any manner by the use or with the aid of artificial lights of any kind. Inasmuch as the above mentioned counties have been omitted from the provisions of Chapter 49, Laws of 1933, the old law is still in effect.

Spearing of the above named fish is permitted in all three zones in the daytime in lakes and streams. except such lakes and streams or portions thereof as are closed to spearing by order of the Director of Game and Fish.

1935
SYNOPSIS OF FISH LAWS
State of Minnesota, Dept. of Conservation
ERLING SWENSON
Director of Game and Fish

GAME FISH

It Is Unlawful:

For a resident over 18 years of age or a non-resident over 16 years of age to fish without a license.

To fish with more than one line or more than one bait, except that three artificial flies may be used.

To fish within fifty feet of any fishway.

To deposit sawdust or refuse or poisonous substance in waters containing fish life.

To buy or sell game fish.

To take or possess at any time, rock or lake sturgeon, shovel-nose or hackelback sturgeon, spoonbill or paddlefish from inland waters.

To take fish in any other manner than by angling with hook and line, except as spearing or netting of certain kinds is expressly permitted.

To take fish from public water closed by Director's Order.

To take fish by means of explosives, drugs, poisons, lime, medicated bait, fish berries, or other deleterious substances, or by nets, tipups, trot lines, wire strings, ropes and cables. Possession of any such substances or contrivances by any person on the waters, shores or islands of this state, shall be presumptive evidence that the same are possessed for use in violation of this section. It shall be unlawful to have in possession fish nets, except minnow nets, landing nets and dip nets and all nets held in stock for sale by dealers, unless tagged and licensed by the Game and Fish Director; nets in possession of licensed commercial fishermen excepted.

18

Government regulations began to restrict the sport of spear fishing as angling grew in popularity. Anglers feared spear fishermen would deplete the game fish populations so they lobbied to limit spear fishing to "trash" fish.

STATE OF MINNESOTA
DEPARTMENT OF CONSERVATION
DIVISION OF GAME AND FISH

N⁰ 18615

1945

FISH HOUSE, DARK HOUSE OR SHELTER LICENSE

Minnesota Statutes 1941, Section 101.25, and Laws Amendatory thereof and Supplementary thereto.

In consideration of the sum of $1.00, receipt of which is hereby acknowledged, license is hereby granted to_____

_Cayl _____ whose postoffice address is _____, and who is the holder of resident or non-resident fishing license to maintain and use for taking fish for domestic or personal use and not for commercial purposes, only one dark house, fish house or shelter while fishing through the ice for the purpose of taking by spearing or angling pickerel, carp, dogfish, buffalofish, whitefish, tullibees, sheepshead, bullheads, catfish, eelpout, garfish, suckers, and redhorse in all waters of this state which have not been closed to fishing in such manner by order of the Commissioner of Conservation, including those waters over which Minnesota has concurrent jurisdiction with other states. Carp caught under this license may be bought and sold at any time.

Licensee must have this license on his person while fishing in a dark house or fish house and license number must be plainly marked on the exterior of the dark house, fish house or shelter.

This license is subject to change as to fees, terms and privileges at any time by legislative action and by order of the Commissioner of Conservation and upon conviction for any violation of any of the provisions of the law relating to this license or relating to wild animals covered by this license, this license shall immediately become null and void and no license of the same kind shall be issued for a period of one year after date of conviction.

This license is not transferable and expires December 31, 1945.

Dated at St. Paul, Minnesota, this ___ day of _____, 1945.

A. M. ____
County Auditor
Pennington County, Minn.

20752 17

_____
Signature of officer or agent authorized to issue license.

States like Minnesota and Wisconsin required licenses for one's darkhouse be posted at all times. These licenses were usually paper, as shown, or small metal tags that could be nailed to the outside of the darkhouse.

Top right: Classic style trout by Harry A. Seymour, Bemus, New York, distinctive anal and dorsal fins, metal fins and leather tail, bored tie line hole and finely detail paint pattern, c.1870. $4000-5000. *Center:* Unknown Lake Chautauqua carver, squared metal fins, uniquely shaped leather tail, painted tack eyes, bored tie line hole, open mouth, and deep gill carving, c.1890. $2000-3000. *Bottom:* Unknown Lake Chautauqua carver, rounded metal fins, leather tail, painted tack eyes, dorsal fin, bar tie line holder, open mouth, and gill carving, c.1900. $3000-4000.

Found in the same barn in western New York on Lake Chautauqua near Bemus Point, these decoys have differences that suggest several unknown makers. *Top:* Obviously patterned after Seymour decoys with dorsal and anal fins, tack eyes, open mouth, gill carving and heavy bar tie line holder, c.1910. $1500-2000. *Center:* Unknown carver created this unusually large 15" northern pike with metal tail and fins, painted eyes and carved mouth, c.1920. $2000-3000. *Bottom:* Unknown maker, distinct square fins, tack eyes, unusually shaped leather tail, and eye screw tie line holder, c.1920. $800-1000.

19

Brown trout decoys, unknown makers, found in same barn near Bemus Point on Lake Chautauqua. *Top to Bottom:* Painted tack eyes with single slash painted in front of the eyes, bored tie line hole, carved mouth and gill and identifying leather tail, c.1910. $800-1000; Painted eyes with single slash painted in front of eyes, anal and dorsal fins, bored tie line hole, carved mouth and gills, and leather tail, c.1910. $800-1000; Patterned from Seymour with square metal fins, leather tail, bored tie line hole, tack eyes with single slash painted in front of eyes, open mouth and deep gill carving, c.1910. $1000-1200; Heavily glazed varnish over original paint decoy with painted tack eyes, squared fins, leather tail, carved mouth and gills, and looped tie line holder, c.1900. $800-1000.

LaCrosse Decoys

Probably no other school of fish decoys was influenced more by the fishing conditions than those produced for use in the Mississippi River near LaCrosse, Wisconsin. Here 'Ole Muddy' spreads out between the towering bluffs on either side of the river as it bends to continue southward along the Wisconsin/ Minnesota border. When LaCrosse was just a booming river port, this stretch of the river widened to form a maze of river islands and massive aquatic weed beds which slowed the river to a gentle current creating a wildlife sanctuary. When the shallow backwaters froze over, local fishermen would take to the ice to spear fish using fish decoys.

It is obvious that these carvers shared ideas and techniques among themselves forming a carving school. Most of the decoys made in this area employed several characteristics that made LaCrosse fish decoy unique from the decoys that were used primarily in lake waters. The LaCrosse river fish decoys are small, rarely measuring more that six inches and often only two or three inches long. River fish were usually painted with muted tones because the gently moving water was always clear. There was no need to added sparkle to attract the game fish. The makers used oil paints in very simple patterns to reproduce the natural appearance of the native fish, most commonly shad, northern pike, sunfish, shiners, chub, bass, and trout. Details were added in the carvings such as gills, mouths, and sometimes scaling. Intricate gill carving often extended to the bottom of the decoy. Using old flatten glass beads for eyes gave a very realistic appearance to the LaCrosse decoy. A straight pin would be run through the bead's hole to attach it to the decoy, creating a pupil.

The body construction of river fish was also consistent. Tiny side fins cut from old tobacco tins or copper were all that was needed to stabilize the decoy in the river's slowed flowage. Anal and dorsal fins were often added just for realism. The tails, whether carved or added in metal, were usually straight. Here again the river flowage alone would create the natural wiggle of a bait fish swimming upstream so there was little need to experiment to recreate the natural movement of a fish. While most LaCrosse carvers added lead weight into the base of their decoys, several makers poured lead ballast into the top of the decoy to hold the tie-line holder adding extra strength to an area subjected to the river's constant force which could pull the holder out. This problem of losing one's tie-line holder was also approached by making the holder an elongated bar allowing the line to slide along the holder. Another common holder was a multiple looped design.

There are undocumented reports that the new game laws instituted in 1928 banned the use of decoys in the LaCrosse area, but, according to locals, the sport of spear fishing continued in this part of the state into the 1930s. The quality of the craftsmanship in the LaCrosse fish is among the best. Their realistic forms and subtle coloration rival the Lake Chautauqua decoy of western New York state and are probably from the same time period.

Bud Hendrickson poses with his fishing buddy in front of his darkhouse on the frozen Mississippi River at LaCrosse, Wisconsin. Note the short spears and low rising shanty, c.1935. *Photo courtesy of Bud Hendrickson.*

LaCrosse fish decoys are usually small, straight-bodied decoys painted in natural muted colors because they were used in free flowing currents of the river that gave the decoy a swimming action and kept the waters clear. The long bar tie line holder seen on most LaCrosse decoys accommodates for the pull of the current. Shown here are assorted LaCrosse decoys, makers unknown, c. 1910-1920. $400-800 each.

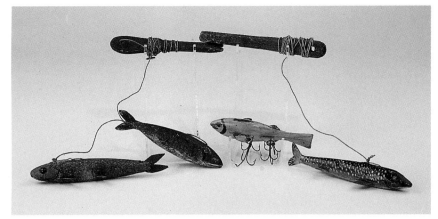

LaCrosse fishermen used a tiny jigging stick often reinforcing the line with a button. *Left to right:* Clarence Zielke, LaCrosse, Wisconsin, c.1910. $400-600; Unknown carver, c.1920. $300-400; Cheater attributed to Bud Beranck, LaCrosse. Locals suggest that hooks were added after fish spearing with decoys was outlawed, c.1910. $300-400; Unknown carver, c.1910. $300-400.

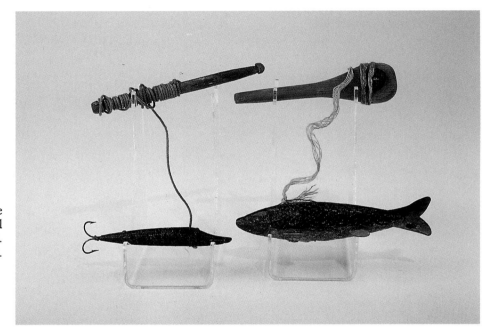

Unknown LaCrosse decoys with typical jigging sticks, c.1900. $300-500 each.

22

Left to right: Unknown LaCrosse northern with unusual jigging stick. Note tiny brass reel, c.1900. $500-750; Monotone shiner decoy by Joe Gohres (1921-1987) LaCrosse. Multiple looped tie line holder, c.1940. $750-1000; Bass decoy by Joe Gohres, c.1940. $750-1000.

Decoys made by Tony Bergans, LaCrosse who ran a boat and guide service off of Green Island during the 1930s. Bregans often leaded the tops of his decoys where he embedded the bar tie line holder, c.1930. $400-500.

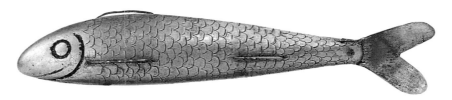

Unknown maker, solid cast aluminum decoy, side fins and tail added, 4", c.1930. $500-750.

23

This half of a cigar box provides a handy decoy holder for tiny decoys measuring 1 1/2 - 2". The northern pike on the far left is highly detailed despite its minuscule size, c.1900. $300-400 each.

MICHIGAN FISH DECOYS

Home to two fish decoy collecting associations, The Great Lakes Fish Decoy Collectors and Carvers Association and The American Fish Decoy Association, Michigan promotes not only the old collectible decoy but also the contemporary decoy makers. Winter spear fishing is still actively practiced here and carvers are providing good working decoys. Although this book is concerned with only old collectibles, it is important to mention that these contemporary decoys are made to be used by serious sportsmen rather than to fool the unsuspecting collector.

As a rule, most Michigan fish decoys are painted in realistic color tones and trout were the most popular. Often used on the large bodied lakes like Lake Michigan, Lake Superior, Lake St. Clair, and Lake Huron, decoys measuring 12"-16" are common in Michigan. Decoys used on the smaller inland lakes are more consistent with decoys from the surrounding states ranging from 4" to 8".

Oscar Peterson, Cadillac, Michigan, carved fish decoys from 1907 until his death in 1951. Although his decoys always retained his signature style, they do vary ranging in length from 4 1/2" to 8". $1500-2000 each.

24

Tom Schroeder (1885-1979), Detroit, Michigan, is considered one of the foremost folk carvers from Michigan. It is believed he only made a dozen or so fish decoys. Walleye, 4 1/2", c.1940. $1000-1500.

Ken Brunning, (1919-1974) Rogers City, Michigan, confined to a wheel chair after an accident, turned to fish decoy making. His decoys are highly detailed and sometimes copied. Look for a fish hook embedded as a tie line holder. Brook trout, 11", c.1950. $3000-4000.

Michigan spearers used decoys measuring 10"-16" to attract whitefish, musky, and sturgeon in the large bodied lakes. *Top:* Robert Pierce, Mt. Clements, speared on Lake St. Clair, 11", c.1936. $500-750. *Center:* Isaac Goulette (1900-1969), New Baltimore, Michigan Blue Herring, 10", c.1925. $500-750. *Bottom:* Unknown Michigan trout, carved body, 11", c.1930. $400-500.

Bud Steward (1912-   ) Flint, Michigan, produced fishing tackle including fish decoys professionally for most of his adult life. His distinctive style has won him national recognition. Sucker, 4", c.1950. $500-750.

Assortment of Michigan fish decoys illustrates the variety of style exhibited by these fine craftsmen, c.1930-1940. $200-300 each.

Minnesota Decoys

The state of Minnesota was home to many of the finest decoy makers known today. The range of style and quality is so great that Minnesota fish decoys defy classification. The isolating nature of this region with its countless lakes and heavy timber forced the decoy makers to rely solely on their own experiences to develop their style and patterns. These men were true folk artists, not trained craftsmen who produced primitive art work, but common men who created a simple tool that helped guaranteed the spear fishermen's success. Because they had to rely upon their own ingenuity and experience to create decoys, their decoys reflect their highly personal interpretation of what a fish looked like and how it moved in the water. The resulting decoys exemplify the strong individualistic personalities that characterized the people who adapted to the harsh conditions of this wilderness. The local hardware store or five & dime was usually the sole source for materials. Decoys were painted with house and model paints. Jewelry beads and tacks became eyes, and Prince Albert tobacco tins or coffee cans became metal fins. Minnesota decoys are a delight in their variety of form and color, ranging from detailed realistic carvings to whimsical abstract fish forms.

The variety of water conditions in the numerous lakes demanded a multitude of colorations. The red and white decoy which was normally a favorite decoy may work great one day on the ice and then fail miserably the next. Most fishermen had a darkhouse box supplied with several different decoys: natural wood, subtle realistically painted, brightly colored abstract designs, and plain red and white. The carvers themselves were often as colorful as their decoys. Most lived in small communities or on secluded lakes. They made decoys for their own use and their reputations spread by word of mouth. Some, however, were able to earn a modest living by selling their decoys at the local bait shop, hardware store, or tavern. Many of the men who are now recognized as major folk artisans traded their work for drinks or created elaborate

pieces as they spent the winter in the county jail for poaching. Only during the last decade have most of these carvers been identified. Some will never be known. Yet the prolific unknown carver cannot be overlooked. Much of the work of these unknown carvers has such strong style that no name is necessary to set it apart from the average decoy.

Unfortunately the great variety among Minnesota decoys makes it easier to mis-identify and mistake newer decoys as old. Often a truly old decoy will look newer than a recent 'fake' because the maker used enamel and marine paints that would withstand frequent submersion. Milk paint is often used on contemporary 'decorator' fish decoys because its flat finish looks ancient. The collector should take care to deal with knowledgeable dealers and to familiarize himself with telltale signs of artificial aging. 'Old Rust' is dark brown and will not rub off on your hand. Fish decoys had to be heavy to sink, and the tie line holder should always be securely attached. Some collectors believe a decoy will hang tail heavy, but this doesn't always hold true.

Fred Lexow (1888-1971), Balsam Lake, Minnesota, moved to the lake after his divorce and devoted his time to his art. Over a period of 30 years, he produced fish decoys, fish plaques, and colored pen and ink drawing to supplement his income. Much of his artwork was traded for food or drinks at the local taverns since he did not drive a car.

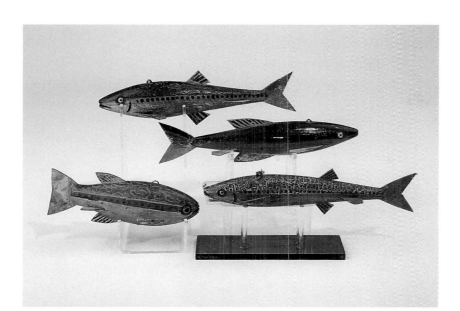

Fred Lexow trout decoys are painted in a strong dotted style that is evident on most of his decoys. His earliest decoys have long slender bodies with sharp angled fins, c.1930. The small fat decoys, like these, are also very desirable, c.1940. The paint on Lexow decoys have a translucent quality because he used transparency paints that his daughter, an employee of Walt Disney studios, supplied. $800-1000 each.

Top: Lexow rarely carved fish species other than trout or silver and red decoys, making this sucker extremely rare, c.1930. $1000-1200. *Center and Bottom:* Classic Lexow trout, c.1940. $600-800.

Decoys by Chet Sawyer will usually have staggered double side fins and a metal tail. The center decoy was painted originally by Fred Lexow during a brief commercial partnership where Lexow painted and Sawyer carved and rigged the decoys, 4"-7", c.1920-1930. $300-500.

Chet Sawyer (1904-1994), Duluth, Minnesota, was a contemporary of Fred Lexow and worked with him in a partnership until he realized it took much longer to made a decoy than it did to paint it, Lexow's share of the work, c.1925.

Without Lexow's help painting, Sawyer's decoys took on simpler paint patterns. His daughter painted some of his decoys copying Lexow's signature dotted paint patterns but Chet painted the majority of his fish grey with red detailing, 5"-10", c.1920-1930. $300-500.

John Ryden, Aitkin, Minnesota, would often spend a summer day sitting in the bank's parking lot hawking hand carved wooden toys, doll furniture fashioned out of tin cans, and fish decoys he made. He turned a shotgun shell crate into a darkhouse box which was found on his old homestead filled with his personal decoys, c.1920. $3000-4000 set.

Ryden decoys measure 3" to 6". His sunfish and crappies are especially pleasing. Most have rippled metal fins and tails with a identifying mouth carving, c.1920. $500-800 each.

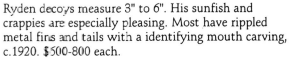

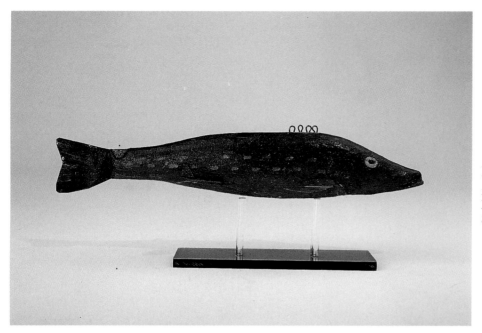

Northern pike carved by Ryden is unusual because its is larger than most Ryden decoys and the only known northern pike, c.1920. $800-1000.

Albert Larson, Palisade, Minnesota, was a good friend and fishing buddy of John Ryden. His darkhouse box include an assortment of wooden and copper fish decoys including an unusual mirrored decoy, c.1940. $200-300 each.

Leroy Howell (1900-1989), Hinkley, Minnesota, produced so many decoys he was sometimes categorized as a manufacturer. In truth, he produced his handmade decoys commercially for over 30 years. His early decoys have a stylized dotted pattern that earned them the nickname "flower" fish, c.1920. $800-1000.

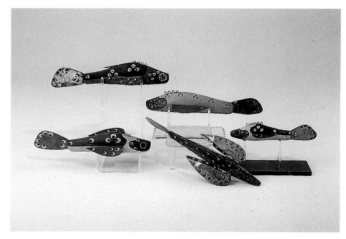

Howell simplified his painting pattern to keep up with the demand for his decoys once he started to market them statewide during the 1930s. *Top:* The sunfish with a wooden tail and penciled scale pattern is a rarity, c.1930. $400-500. *Bottom:* Commercial Howell decoys are usually painted with a simple two color design, c.1940. $300-400.

Ray Thompson (1887-1966), Park Rapids, Minnesota, took great pains to detail his decoy down to carving the tongue and adding tiny metal teeth. His decoys are extremely rare, c.1930. $4000-5000.

Frank Mizera (1898-1969) worked as a fishing guide out of Ely, Minnesota most of his life and fished commercially, selling smoked fish to tourists in neighboring Boundary Waters communities. He supplemented this income by making decoys and lures which were distributed as far south as the Twin Cities.

Top: Red & white decoys are very common in Minnesota because they work! c.1940. $200-300. *Bottom:* Mizera fish decoys that are painted with little fish are the most collectible of his work, c.1930. $300-500.

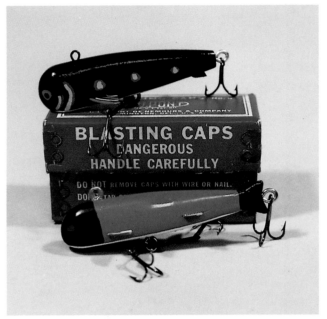

Mizera packaged his fishing lures in old blasting cap boxes from the taganite mines in the local iron range, c.1940. $150-200.

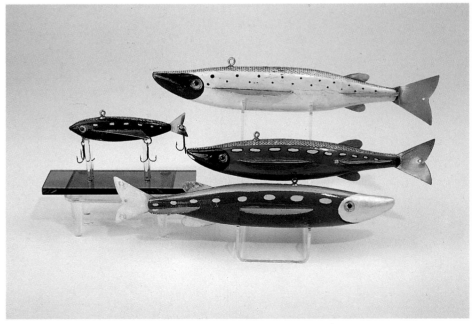

Ernest Newman (1908-1976), Carlton, Minnesota, produced fish decoys and lures as a hobby for 50 years. Using only the finest tackle paints and seasoned redwood, his decoys aged very well. Relying on word of mouth, his production was limited to supply local fishermen, c.1940. $300-500 each.

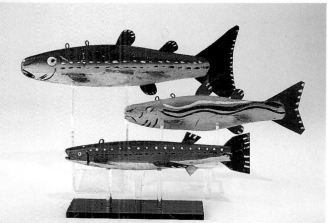

Pearl Bethel is noted for his jointed fish decoys. Early examples like these have rubber hinges; later models utilize metal hinges and are still being produced by Pearl's son Lawrence, 9", c.1930. $300-500 each.

The Bethel brothers, Pearl (1894-1960) and Cyril (1900-1980) both lived in Park Rapids, Minnesota and produced fish decoys. *Top:* Pearl Bethel, trout, 10", c.1930. $200-300. *Center:* Pearl Bethel, abstract design, 8", c.1930. $200-300. *Bottom:* Cyril Bethel, 8", c.1920. $150-200.

Chuck Hall (1908-1995), Barnum, Minnesota, was one of many Minnesotans who literally lived off the land most of their lives. Hunting, fishing and gardening supported his family. Selling his fish decoys at the local hardware store also helped.

A darkhouse box like this one owned by Chuck Hall usually stored a variety of fish decoys. Hall would use any scrap that was available to fashion his decoys and used paint-by-numbers set paints bought at the 5 & 10 cent store and cheap paint brushes. Hardly the makings of fine art, yet his decoys are recognized as some of the finest, 4"- 6", c.1920. $400-600 each.

Raymond Stotz (1897-1976), Cleveland, Minnesota, painted his decoys in abstract and realistic designs, perch, 6"- 8", c.1920. $300-500 each.

This early Stotz decoy is a good example of the level of expertise Stotz practiced when he painted his decoys. Each scale is denoted with fine black brush strokes, 9", c.1910. $800-1000.

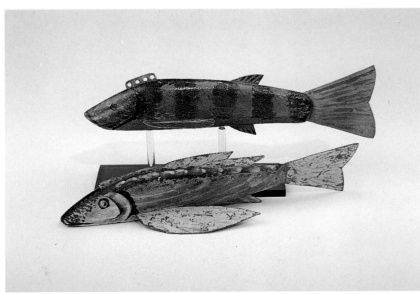

The Faue brothers, William (1878-1950) and Otto (1881-1954) carved decoys using the same patterns except Otto usually added four side fins and William used two. Shown are William Faue decoys, realistic and abstract styles, 7", c.1930. $800-1000 each.

John Greer carried decoys out to the darkhouse in this case that he decorated when he guided on Mille Lacs, near Garrison, Minnesota, 4"- 8", c.1920. $300-400 each.

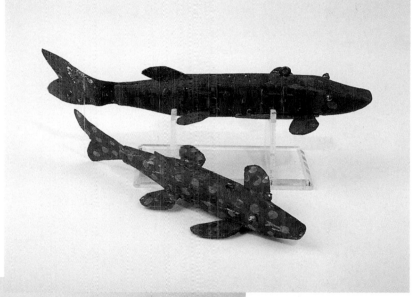

Frank Achop, Walker, Minnesota, 5"- 7", c.1930. $75-100.

Wilbur Peterson, Baxter, Minnesota, 4"- 7", c.1930. $400-600 each.

William "Slow" Batter (1882-1957), Little Falls, Minnesota, carved his decoys when he was on duty in the city fire house. For years his decoys had been misidentified as being made by a Harry Blancherd. *Photo courtesy of Heidi Price.*

Slow Batter's decoys all display a distinctive lower lip carving. They range in size from tiny 1 1/2" red & white's to 20" store display models, c.1930. $400-500 each.

The Lacni brothers both made their fish decoys very thin with no side fins. *Top:* Joseph Lacni, Virginia, Minnesota, crappie, 4", c.1920. $300-500. *Bottom:* Stephen Lacni, Virginia, Minnesota, crappie silhouette, 8", c.1920. $250-400.

Left: Merle Falstad, Park Rapids, Minnesota, bullhead, 7", c.1950. $800-1000. *Right:* Otto Bishop, Osage, Minnesota, bullhead, 6 1/4", c.1940. $300-500.

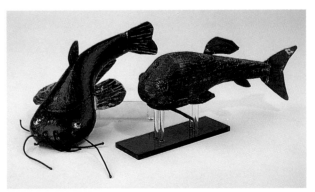

Albert Morris, Grand Rapids, Minnesota, abstract
sunfish, 4", c.1920. $400-500.

Fred Johnson, Bovey, Minnesota, exceptional abstract
decoys, c.1930. $300-400 each.

Charles Engles, Minnesota, northern pike, 5", c.1920.
$300-400. *Courtesy of private collection.*

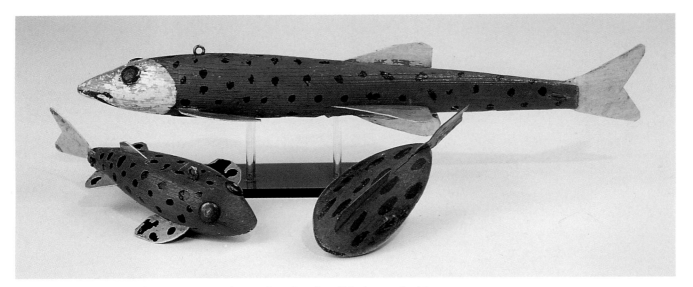

Ivan Amist, Grand Rapids, Minnesota, who made only a few fish decoys for his own use, utilized a simple dotted pattern to decorate his decoys. *Lower right:* Interesting tadpole decoy by Amist, 4"- 12", c.1920. $400-500.

Several of these thin abstract decoys have been found in the Brainerd, Minnesota area. Formerly attributed to Marion Butcher, they were carved by Art Boelter, Le Sueur, Minnesota, and sold exclusively through Smallis Bait Shop, Minneapolis. 6", c.1930. $300-500 each.

Another decoy maker that is believed to be misidentified is Fred Gibbon. His decoys were found in St. Cloud and sold by a relative who wished to protect his identity. At any rate they are exception decoys, 4"-7", c.1940. $500-700 each.

This unknown sunfish has a strong scandinavian influence from the quality wood crafting where the tail was inset to the bold abstract paint pattern done in primary colors. Found in Park Rapids, Minnesota area, 6 1/2", c.1920. $800-1000.

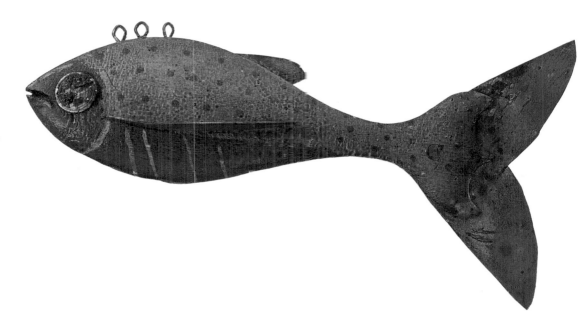

Found in the Mille Lacs, Minnesota area, this unknown decoy is exceptional because it depicts a perch stealing an egg off a spawning bed, 6", c.1920. $600-800.

Although this large unknown sunfish has obvious wear and some damage, its size and form make it a very collectible piece, 8", c.1920. $500-700.

39

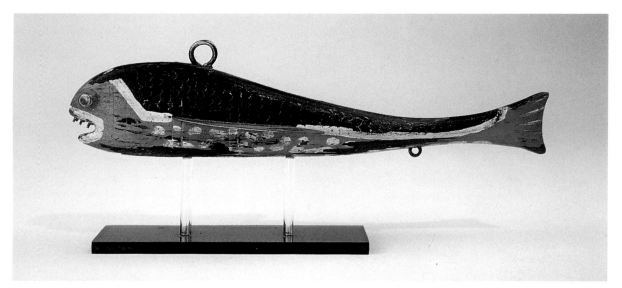

One wonders what this unknown carver from the Grand Rapids area was imagining when he created this fanciful decoy, 7", c.1920. $200-300.

Unknown maker, Grand Rapids, Minnesota, 10", c.1920. $300-500.

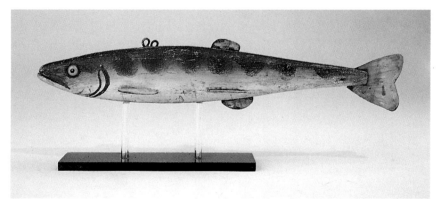

Unknown maker, Bovey, Minnesota, perch, 8", c.1930. $300-500.

This perch by an unknown maker from Bovey, Minnesota, exhibits quality workmanship and a steady hand. Individual scales are indicated with fine black paint strokes, 11", c.1920. $500-700.

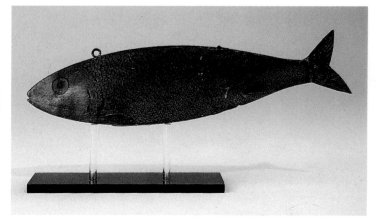

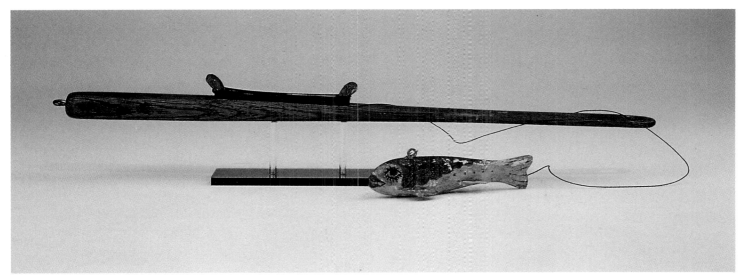

This little unknown fish decoy is all decked out with a
pretty face to attract the "big one", 4", c.1930. $200-300.

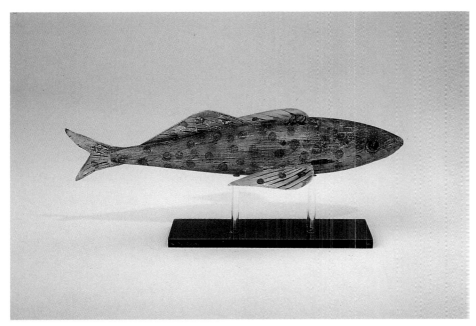

The flowing lines and "angel fins" add
to the value of this unknown decoy
from Bovey, Minnesota, 7", c.1930.
$300-500.

Unknown maker, Crosslake, Minnesota, northern pike, 10", c.1930. $400-
500.

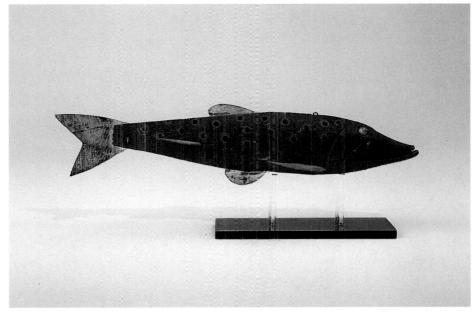

41

Unknown maker, Walker, Minnesota, northern pike, 7",
c.1920. $300-400.

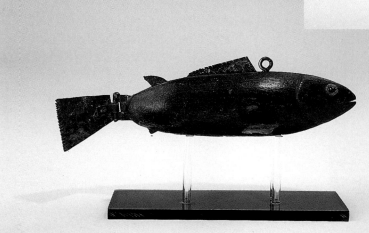

Unknown maker, Grand Rapids, Minnesota. Natural
finish with copper fins and movable tail, 5", c.1920.
$400-500.

This unknown fish decoy has movable side fins which
created a rippling effect when the decoy was drawn
through the water, Grand Rapids, 6 1/2", c.1930. $400-
500.

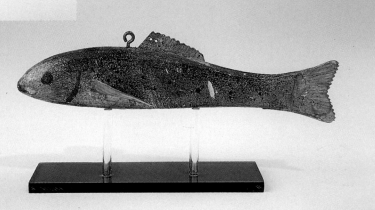

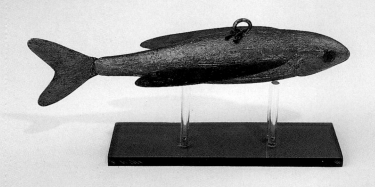

Metallic gold paint adds luster that would hopefully
catch the glint of the refractured sunlight, making it
more appealing to a passing fish, Grand Rapids, Minnesota, 5", c.1920. $200-300.

Double-sided frog bait sign hung in Grand Rapids bait shop, 12" x 29", c.1940. $200-300.

Frogs and other critters were another addition to the fish decoy makers pallet. Their interesting form spurred the imagination of the carver and the collector. Pictured are assorted frog decoys from Minnesota and Wisconsin, 2"-7", c.1930-40. $400-500 each.

43

Fred Lexow, Balsam Lake, Minnesota, was one of the few carvers who produced crawfish decoys. The large metal crawfish have weighted wooden bodies, 4"-5", c.1940. $300-400.

Nicknamed the Mille Lacs frog, these decoys are all attributed to Fred Waltham, Brainerd, Minnesota, who worked for Burlington Railroad and made fish with his brother and father, 4"-7", c.1930-40. Fish: $200-300 each. Frogs: $500-700 each.

44

Art E. Storrs, LeCenter, Minnesota, carved frog decoys commercially from 1930 to 1950. *Left to right:* Early style with notched fins, c.1930. $250-300; Later commercial model, c.1950. $150-200; Middle career model still has rounded hand-cut fins, c.1940. $200-250.

Wilbur Peterson, Baxter, Minnesota, frog, c.1935. $500-700.

John Tax, Osakis, Minnesota, one of the premier folk artists from the state, produced waterfowl decoys, fish and frog decoys and delightful folk pieces like this bass birdhouse which has a tiny opening for a wren in its mouth. Frog: 6", c.1930. $500-700. *Courtesy of private collection.* Fish: 5", c.1940. $300-500. Birdhouse: 16", c.1950. $3000-4000.

Top: Charles Slectha (1896-1974), Minneapolis, Minnesota, 10 1/2", c.1930. $500-700. *Lower left:* International Harvester employee produced this squared-edged decoy, 11", c.1940. $400-600. *Lower right:* Thomas J. Downing (1886-1991), Minneapolis, Minnesota, sunfish, 4", c.1930. $750-1000.

Merril Booth (1892-1966), Minneapolis, Minnesota, shown at his work bench soldering together one of his copper fish decoys, c.1950.

Top: Merril Booth, Minneapolis, Minnesota, 10 1/2", c.1940. $400-600. *Bottom, left to right:* Unknown sand-casted solid sunfish, 7", c.1950. $300-400; Hollow beaver decoy, 8", c.1950. $500-700; Unknown silhouette, northern pike, 6", c.1940. $150-200; Primitive unknown hollow, 10", c.1940. $150-200.

45

Fishermen are an ingenious sort. This fellow raided his wife's kitchen for a hand-mixer which he used to slowly turn his Booth fish decoy in the water. *Photo courtesy of John Banholzer.*

Top left: Merril Booth, Minneapolis, Minnesota, 10", c.1940. $400-500. *Top right:* Charles Slectha, Minneapolis, Minnesota, 10", c.1940. $400-500. *Lower left:* Unknown maker, wooden head inlaid with copper scales, 7", c.1930. $150-200. *Lower right:* Turtle decoy, unknown maker, 4", c.1940. $500-600.

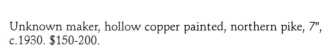

Unknown maker, hollow copper painted, northern pike, 7", c.1930. $150-200.

John Emerson, Superior, Wisconsin, made excellent examples of cast metal decoys shown here with a single wooden sunfish (largest decoy), his customized jigging stick, and his darkhouse box, 2"- 4". $200-300 each.

FACTORY DECOYS

Although the growing fraternity of angling fishermen frowned upon the spear fisherman, most of the major tackle companies offered a limited line of spearing decoys. The Jim Heddon & Sons Tackle Company, Dowagiac, Wisconsin offered several variations of a wooden fish decoy as well as a plastic fish decoy in their effort to keep up with the latest trends in tackle equipment. They made every effort to be first in their field; so it is not surprising that Heddon offered the Heddon Ice Minnow #400 as early as 1913 in an illustrated full color inset in the H.H. Michaelson, New York City, Sporting Goods Catalog.

During the years Heddon produced fish decoys, they modified their decoy pattern to include metal tailed decoys and two styles of side fins. In their 1930 catalog, Heddon announced a new line of "Spook" baits made of a transparent plastic called "Heddylin" with life-like finish that resembled fish flesh. The Ice Spook decoy which would replace the wooden decoy had a silhouetted body mounted on an over-sized lead belly weight which was stamped "HEDDON ICE SPOOK". Although the Ice Spook was distributed for a number of years it is not known to have been illustrated in any of the company's catalogs. Like many of the plastic baits of this era, the Ice Spook had a tendency to disintegrate when stored in a tackle box. For this reason few Ice Spooks have survived and they are highly collectible even though they are plastic. All of the Heddon fish decoys are rare because of their limited production.

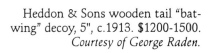

Color insert from the *1913 H.H. Michaelson Sporting Goods catalog*, New York, New York, illustrating the Heddon "Dowagiac" decoy ice minnow.

Heddon & Sons wooden tail "batwing" decoy, 5", c.1913. $1200-1500. *Courtesy of George Raden.*

Prototype Heddon & Sons fish decoy, never cataloged, 8",
c.1910. $2500-3000. *Courtesy of private collection.*

James Heddon & Sons Tackle
Company, Dowagiac, Michigan. *Top
left:* Three top decoys, Ice Decoy
Minnow #400, 4 3/8" double side
fins, c.1920. $400-500 each. *Lower
left:* Ice-Spook #450, plastic, 5",
c.1935. $250-300. *Top right:* Two top
decoys, Ice Decoy Minnow #400, 4
3/8" double side fins, c.1920. $400-
500. *Lower right:* Spearing Decoy
"Bat-Wing", 4 1/4".c.1913. $600-700.

48

The patented (c.1892) soft rubber minnow that was the staple of the Pflueger Bait Company (Enterprise Manufacturing Company) was easily adapted into a fish decoy. Earliest models simply had a tie-line holder added to the dorsal fin of the minnow. Later a cut was made into the body to allow a metal piece to be slid through it to form two perpendicular side fins that help stabilize the decoy in the water. Pflueger's fish decoy had details such as eyes, gill, scales and an open mouth molded directly into it. Though the decoys were made of soft rubber, they harden with age and became very brittle so few survived. Pflueger also offered a wooden fish decoy in its pre-1900 catalog although it was

not pictured. Like the company's "wooden minnow" lures, this decoy was made of selected stock shaped into a streamlined finless form with glass eyes and a metal tail. The decoy was coated with eight to twelve coats of a "Special Elastic, indestructible and water proof, Porcelain Enamel" which came in two color patterns identical to the rubber decoy's —decorated (perch) and plain silver that were offered in luminous and non-luminous paint. The new luminous paint offered by Pflueger was described as a phosphorescent glow, not a brilliant shine but just enough to represent the unusual glittering scales of a live fish in the water. The Pflueger wooden decoy also came in two sizes: 3 1/2 and 5 inches.

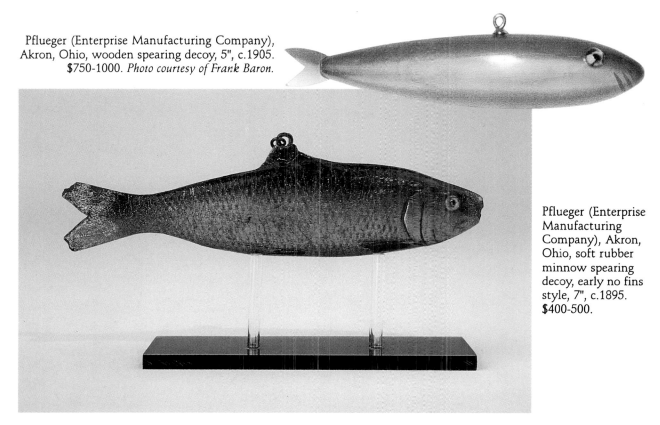

Pflueger (Enterprise Manufacturing Company), Akron, Ohio, wooden spearing decoy, 5", c.1905. $750-1000. *Photo courtesy of Frank Baron.*

Pflueger (Enterprise Manufacturing Company), Akron, Ohio, soft rubber minnow spearing decoy, early no fins style, 7", c.1895. $400-500.

The history of the PawPaw Company is closely tied into that of the Moonlight Bait Company started in 1906 by Horace Ball and Charles Varney of Paw Paw, Michigan which offered fish decoys. In 1927 Moonlight employees Floyd Phelps and Clyde Sinclair patented a silver flashing feature which would be used on the Moonlight Bait Company's fish decoys. When the Moonlight Bait Company had began the transition into the PawPaw Bait Company which was incorporated in 1935 with Sinclair as the president, the manufacturing of fish decoys continued. Next to Heddon & Sons, the PawPaw Bait Company offered the greatest variety of fish decoys to their customers, producing three styles of wooden fish decoys in a wide variety of colors with or without a finishing coating of silver glitter. The smaller decoys measuring 2 3\4 inches and 5 inches had carved wooden tails, four side fins and a dorsal fin. Hardware included a single nickel eye screw

mounted ahead of the dorsal fin and a metal pin to protect the nose. All PawPaw decoys can be differentiated from the earlier Moonlight decoys by their tack eyes which were

Moonlight/Paw Paw Bait Company, Paw Paw, Michigan, ice spearing decoys in various color patterns, 5"-7", c.1920-30. $300-400 each.

inserted prior to applying the multiple coatings of enamel found on all the company's baits. The other style decoy was longer, 7 inches, with a sleeker body form which was finished off with a metal tail. These decoys had similar hardware and fin placement to the smaller versions.

49

In their effort to supply the needs of every fisherman, the South Bend Bait Company, South Bend, Indiana, offered fish decoys for limited distribution in the northern states during the early 1900s. South Bend introduced an ice spearing decoy in their 1923-24 trade catalog. The decoy was simply a glass eyed bait body with an eye screw added to its back. Cataloged as the 5 1\4" #258SF (green scale) and #258RHA (red head/ aluminum body), the South Bend ice decoy was not known to have been cataloged elsewhere. The decoy's lack of fins and tail combined with its simple design and paint pattern causes inexperienced collectors to believe they were simply lures without hooks.

South Bend Bait Company, South Bend, Indiana, South Bend Minnow, 5 1/4", c.1920. $400-600. *Photo courtesy of Frank Baron.*

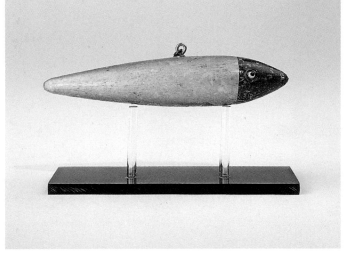

South Bend Bait Company, South Bend, Indiana, South Bend Minnow, Green scale #258SF, Red head/ silver body #258RHA, 5 1/4", c.1920. $400-600. *Photo courtesy of Frank Baron.*

50

Creek Chub Bait Company, Garret, Indiana, wooden spearing decoy, 5", "Dace" color pattern, c.1905. $750-1000. *Photo courtesy of Frank Baron.*

The K & E Company, Hastings, Michigan is one of the few commercial bait companies that still manufactures fish decoys. Their Ice King brand winter spearing decoy was first produced in wood by the Bear Creek Bait Company in Kaleva, Michigan in 1946. Sometime during the 1950s the company switched to a plastic design with metal fins and later to a solid plastic construction. The current K & E Company's Ice King decoy is a hollow plastic decoy.

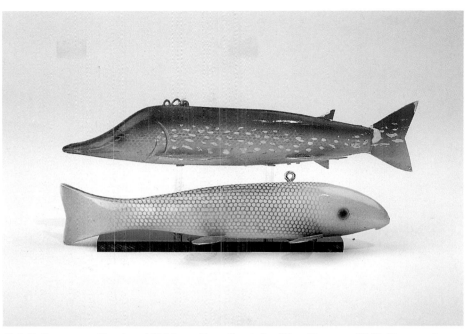

K & E Company, Hasting, Michigan, Bear Creek Ice King Decoy, c.1940. *Top:* northern pike, 7 1/4". $300-400 *Bottom:* sucker, 6 3/4". $300-400.

There were several smaller cottage industries which commercially marketed fish decoys. The Randall decoy was produced in Wilmar Minnesota and is easily identified by the cast lead belly weight which included side fins that was screwed to the decoy. Earliest examples of Randall decoys had wooden tails and sometimes a curved body. The Randall decoys were spray painted in a variety of interesting paint patterns prior to 1960. Around this time Randall switched to a solid cast metal fish decoy. George Herter, Waseca, Minnesota did not make decoys but his company distributed hunting and fishing equipment under their own label for years. The Herter's fish decoy was a streamlined design with glass eyes, a multiple tie line holder, double side fins, and a metal tail.

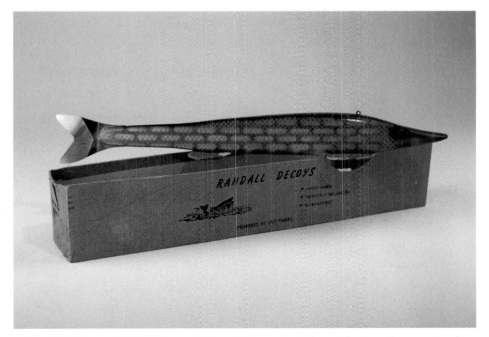

Randall Decoys & Fish Spears, Wilmar, Minnesota, "Come-On" northern, natural pickerel #R 500, 16", c.1940. $300-400.

Herter's Manufacturers, Waseca, Minnesota, marketed "trade" decoys produced by an unknown company, c.1940. *Top:* Perch, 7 1/4". $400-500. *Lower left:* Sunfish, 5 3/4". $400-500. *Lower right:* Perch, 5 1/4". $400-500.

Randall decoys can be worked either fast or slow by just bending the back fins slightly: bend fin down for fast—up for slow. Large sizes work very well alone or with a small decoy or a live bait. This dual combination tends to slow down the fish giving the fisherman a much better chance.

All decoys are made of select wood with casted lead fins.

Deluxe Decoy

Four popular sizes — ten attractive colors:

Fact. No.	Size	List	
R125	6"	$1.25	*8756
R150	8"	1.50	*8901
R175	10"	1.75	*21056
R200	12"	2.00	*21201

Randall Decoys & Fish Spears, Wilmar, Minnesota, original catalog flyer, c.1940. $25-50.

DELUXE DECOYS by Randall
WILLMAR, MINNESOTA

Sunfish

CRAPPIE RSF 135

BLUEGILL RSF 135

Has a lazy carefree action. Sunfish have long been a favorite dish for large northerns. Comes in crappie or bluegill finishes.

Fact. No.	Size	List	
RSF135	5"	$1.35	*9812

Golden Sucker

Has a slow easy action that suggests a tempting meal to any passing northern. Natural finish only.

Fact. No.	Size	List	
RS150	6"	$1.50	*8901
RS175	8"	1.75	*21056
RS200	10"	2.00	*31201
RS250	12"	2.50	*41501

"Come On" Northern

Natural Pickerel R 500

Red Head Pickerel R 500

Works equally well alone or as a "come-on" with a smaller decoy or live bait. Red head or natural finishes only.

Fact. No.	Size	List	
R500	16"	$4.95	*53006

It is not so surprising that the tackle companies did not cater extensively to the ice spearing fisherman. Angling fishermen were convinced that winter spearing fish would destroy the game fish populations. The outdoor magazines gave little or no coverage to the sport of spear fishing. Even Ernest Pflueger seemed to be snubbing the spear fisherman in his catalog with the following quote: "It (Pflueger's Decoy Minnow) furnishes great sport to those that indulge in this class of fishing." In all fairness, the fish decoy had a very limited marketing base since only the hearty could practice the sport in the northernmost states. Although the demands of commercial mass production restricted the creativeness of these decoys, their air-brushed paint patterns are pleasing and worthy of collecting. Any of the tackle companies' decoys are very collectible because of their rarity and appeal to both tackle and decoy collectors.

CHAPTER 2
ICE STICKS AND SPEARS

Winter fishing required an entirely different sort of equipment. Obviously there was no need for long casting rods or casting reels. A short rod and simple line holder would do for ice fishing and this is what most fishermen used. Yet there are wonderfully creative sticks that were made by men who wanted something a little special. The collectible ice fishing stick is a combination walking cane with a sharp metal point that would stick into the ice

to steady one's pace and to hold the stick upright when not in use, a line holder and a fishing rod.

Another unique piece of equipment for the ice fisherman was his jigging stick. A short rod, usually wooden because metal would get too cold to hold, was used to suspend the fish decoy through the fisherman's hole in the ice. Some type of line holder was often incorporated into the collectible jigging stick. The decoy was worked in the water by moving the stick with slight wrist movements thus the name "jigging stick". Many fisherman used a small branch or stick, but as one's desire to have something better than the next guy took over, fancy sticks were shaped, painted, and sometimes carved and inscribed.

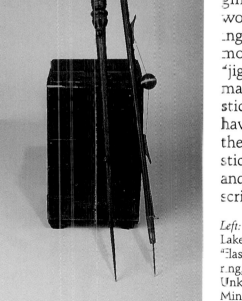

Left: Unknown maker, Big Sandy Lake, McGregor, Minnesota, hollow "flask" handle, walnut with brass ring, c.1930. $200-300. *Right:* Unknown maker, Grand Rapids, Minnesota, painted with metal fittings, c.1930. $200-300.

Assorted jigging sticks. *Top:* Unknown maker, Walker, Minnesota, duck head, 20", c.1940. $400-500. *Lower left to right:* John Emerson, Superior, Wisconsin, painted, 7", c.1920. $75-100; Typical hand made stick, pine, 15". $35-50; Unknown, Aitkin, Minnesota, blue milk paint, 15", c.1930. $75-100.

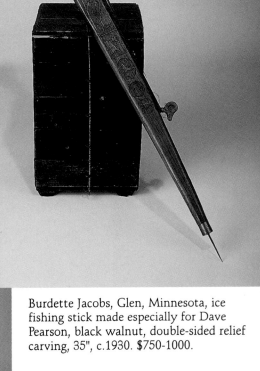

Left to right: William Faue, Hanover, Minnesota, "Kissing Fish" fishing stick, white cedar, jeweled eyes, 32", c.1930. $1000-1500; William Faue painted triple fish fishing stick, exceptional piece, 32", c.1920. $1500-2000; William Faue, "Kissing fish" fishing stick, white cedar, bead eyes, 32". $1000-1500.

Burdette Jacobs, Glen, Minnesota, ice sticks, white cedar double-sided relief carving. *Left:* Miniature 12", c.1940. $300-500. *Right:* Full sized sticks, 35", c.1940. $300-500 each.

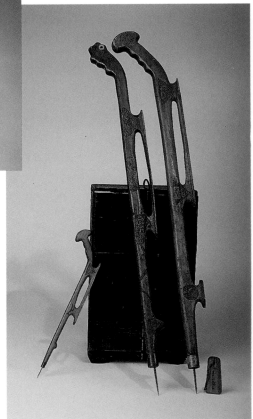

Burdette Jacobs, Glen, Minnesota, ice fishing stick made especially for Dave Pearson, black walnut, double-sided relief carving, 35", c.1930. $750-1000.

The spear fishermen used a trident usually with five to seven razor-sharp barb tines. These spears had weighted heads and a balanced shaft so they would slide swiftly and straight through the water. Spear designs range for crude homemade spear heads attached to broom handles to fine chrome spears forged by experience metalsmiths. There were few manufacturers who produced spears but most commercial spears were forged by local blacksmiths. Only recently has the tedious documentation on the individual spear craftsmen begun with Marcel Saliva's book *Ice Fishing Spears* because most collectors only purchased spears to round off their ice decoy collections. Spear styling varied according to the type of fish being speared. Before government regulations small spear heads were used to harvest small game fish, like bass and pan fish. When the fisherman was limited to large northern pike and sturgeon, he relied on a larger heavy spear. Wisconsin sturgeon ice fishermen still use a unique breakaway spear head which is attached to the shaft with a pin that will break and allow the fish to swim tether until it tires. The handle was retrieved separately. Every spearer hopes to strike his fish directly behind its head for this paralyzes the fish making it easy to retrieve.

55

Proud spears became victims of public outrage fueled by fears of sports anglers who foretold the lost of game fish in the northern lakes because of winter spearing, Minnesota, c.1950. *Photo courtesy of John Banholzer.*

Spear size was also determined by the depth of the water. LaCrosse, Wisconsin fishermen who commonly speared in shallow river back waters use short three to four foot spears. The spears from this region are usually one-piece tridents with finely crafted handles. Spears used on deep lakes had to be heavier and required a much longer shaft, often measuring over 5 feet. Randall Decoys & Spear Company from Wilmar, Minnesota marketed several styles of spears including spear heads sold individually or with custom balanced handles.

Unknown maker, Northern Minnesota, part of a two-piece set, nine razor-sharp tines are set into heavy metal heads, painted, with painted tine shield, 46", c.1920. $500-700.

Unknown maker, Northern Minnesota, part of two-piece set. Seven tine for smaller game fish, red tine shield (not shown), 46", c.1920. $500-700.

Deluxe
BALANCED SPEARS

5 TINE

Width — 5⅜"
Tine Length — 7⅝"
¼" Hi Carbon Steel
5/16" Center Tine
Length of Head — 20"
Overall Length — 60"
2½-Lb. Weighted Head
1 1/16 Tubular Handle
R895   List $8.95   *65402

Rope goes inside handle making a nice smooth connection that will not splash or deflect flight of spear.

5 TINE

Width — 5⅜"
Tine Length — 7⅝"
¼" Hi Carbon Steel
5/16" Center Tine
With ¼" Solid Handle
Weight 2½ Lbs. (Approx.)
5595   List $5.95   *43602

STANDARD SPEARS

7 TINE

Width — 7⅛"
Tine Length — 7⅝"
¼" Hi Carbon Steel
5/16" Center Tine
Length of Head — 22"
Overall Length — 60"
2½-Lb. Weighted Head
1 1/16 Tubular Handle
R1195   List $11.95   *87204

7 TINE

Width — 7⅛"
Length of Tine — 7⅝"
¼" Hi Carbon Steel
5/16" Center Tine
With ¼" Solid Handle
Weight 3 Lbs. (Approx.)
5795   List $7.95   *54803

All Spears shown are breakdown models.

Randall
DECOYS & FISH SPEARS
WILLMAR, MINNESOTA

Randall Decoys And Spears, Wilmar, Minnesota, supplied spears with a fine cast spear head which could be bought with or without a weight shaft. c.1930-50.

Unknown Minnesota maker, hollow metal handle welded to 6 tine head, 60", c.1930. $300-500.

Unknown Minnesota maker, long shafted spear head, wooden handle, 5 tine, 40", c.1930. $150-200.

Unknown Minnesota maker, hand forged one-piece metal construction, 8 tine, 59", c.1930. $300-500.

57

Unknown Minnesota maker, crude wood handle fitted into long shaft spear head, 6 tine, 54", c.1920. $150-200.

Unknown Minnesota maker, square spear head, 7 tine, 49", c.1920. $200-300.

Unknown maker, LaCrosse, Wisconsin, one-piece metal construction with wood cap and tine shield, 5 tine, 38", c.1910. $150-200.

Unknown maker, LaCrosse, Wisconsin, long shafted spear head with finely grained wooden handle, 5 tine, 38", c.1910. $200-300.

Unknown LaCrosse, Wisconsin, tang shaft head (middle tang is extension of the handle), 5 tine, 42", c.1920. $200-300.

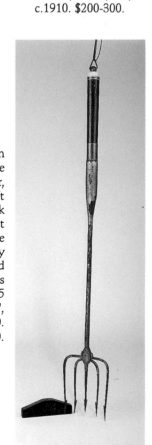

Unknown LaCrosse maker, tang shaft head, black walnut handle with ivory finial and brass fittings, 5 tine, 38", c.1900. $500-700.

Unknown maker, LaCrosse, Wisconsin, fine 6 tine spear head for small game fish, black walnut handle with brass fittings, 38", c.1900. $500-700.

Long shafted spear head with white pine handle, 5 tine, 38", c.1910. $200-300.

Unknown maker, LaCrosse, Wisconsin, 5 tine, metal handle cap has reinforcing metal rings inlaid into the wooden handle, 38", c.1910. $300-400.

CHAPTER 3
LURES

Fishing lures are probably the most actively collected fishing paraphernalia. This is a direct result of a strong organization of the lure collectors in the National Fishing Lure Collectors Club. This club holds a yearly national show and numerous sanctioned regional shows where it polices its 4,000 plus membership to discourage misrepresentation of any lures. The field of fishing lures is the most complicated because millions of lures were mass produced. Many styles were produced with different types of hardware and in numerous color patterns, all traits that determine the value of a particular lure. There are books on the market that define the different lures. Thus, this chapter will concentrate on some of the more collectible examples produced by the major tackle companies, handmade lures, and boxed baits. This is by no means comprehensive coverage, but an overview of the variety of the hobby.

Collecting baits is a great hobby. Like stamps collecting, there is a broad range of values and almost endless variety. A youngster can start collecting early plastic and novelty baits in a five and ten dollar range and can advance into higher price lures as his hobby matures. Serious collectors will find investment quality baits available starting around three hundred dollars. The secret of tackle collecting is condition-condition- condition! Any minor wear affects the value of any bait. Good early baits in their original boxes are considered premiums. In some cases, the box is actually worth more than the lure.

The Heddon Tackle Company, Dowagiac, Wisconsin is a good place to start a lure collection. Introduced in 1898 and still produced by Pardo Company, Arkansas, Heddon Tackle offers hundreds of different style baits. Most of their baits are clearly marked, often with the bait's name imprinted on the belly of the lure. The hardware such as spinners, lips, and side fins is also usually marked. Over the years, the company used three distinct styles of hardware to attach their hooks: Cup-rig, L-rig and two-piece "Toilet Seat" rig which are helpful in dating the various baits. The quality and variety of their product line is a delight to the collector. In addition to developing a wide selection of casting, fly fishing, and trolling baits, Heddon also offered spearing decoys for the ice fishermen. The Heddons were active fishermen and prided themselves in providing fishermen with tackle that kept up with the latest trend in tackle equipment. They made very effort to be first in their field and offered an ever-increasing number of baits. Heddon baits have high quality paint patterns that were air-brushed in multiple layers. Heddon also supplied special paint patterns on request, so unique one-of-a-kind pieces do exist.

Assorted collectible buttons and fishing license buttons $15-25. *Center:* National Fishing Lure Collectors Club, charter patch, c.1976. $25-50.

59

Top left: Earliest known style Heddon #150, brass hardware, high slant forehead, 3 1/2", c.1906. $600-800. *Center left:* Heddon Double-Dummy Minnow #1500, perch, 3", c.1913. $500-700. *Bottom:* Heddon Double-Dummy #1500, carnival, 3", c.1913. $500-700. *Center right:* A.F. Bingenheimer, Milwaukee, Wisconsin, Single Hook Bucktail Minnow, metallic gold, 1 1/2", c.1906. $500-750. *Top right:* Wm. Shakespeare, Kalamazoo, Michigan, Wood Revolution, silver, 3 1/2", c.1900. $800-1000.

Catalog covers, James Heddon & Sons Tackle Company, Dowagiac, Michigan. c.1954-55.

60

Heddon's "Dowagiac" Minnows

NO. 175 (FANCY BACK)

"DOWAGIAC" MINNOW, NO. 175 SERIES

Have two spinners and three special No. 1-0 extra strong nickel plated treble hooks, which hold fish weighing as high as fifty pounds.; length of body 3½ inches.

Weight, approximately 18 pwts.; length of body 3½ inches.

Furnished in the following variety of beautifully blended colors: No. 175, Fancy Green back, White belly; No. 176, Rainbow Colors; No. 177, White body with Slate Colored back.

No. 200 (SPECIAL)

"DOWAGIAC" MINNOW, NO. 200 SPECIAL "EXPERT"

The original "DOWAGIAC" Surface Casting or skittering Bait without revolving parts; semi-weedless with two trebles on bottom and one at tail. Weight 14 pwts.

Furnished in White Body with Nickeled Collar and Blue snout.

No. 200 (SPECIAL LUMINOUS OR MOONLIGHT)

For night fishing. Same as No. 200 Special Expert shown above.

No. 200 (SPECIAL FROG)

Same as No. 200 Special Expert shown above excepting has imitation Frog finish.

H. H. Michaelson Sporting Goods, New York, New York catalog pages illustrating Heddon "Dowagiac" Minnow. c.1913.

Heddon's "Dowagiac" Minnows

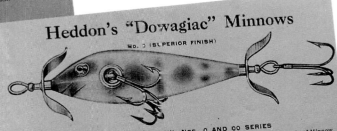

NO. 0 (SUPERIOR FINISH)

"DOWAGIAC" MINNOW, NOS. 0 AND 00 SERIES

This is a new design with five flat surfaces and side hooks mounted on a ridge with body of Minnow sloping away from the hooks, leaving them in the clearest possible position for efficiency. Two spinners, extra strong "DOWAGIAC" design nickel plated treble hooks, supplied in either three treble hook pattern or five treble hook pattern weighs 13 pwts., length of body 3 inches.

Colors No. 0, White Body, Red and Green Decorations. No. 01, Yellow body, Red, Green and Black Decorations. No. 02, Red Body with Black Decorations.

Five treble hook pattern weighs 16 pwts., length of body 3 1-2 inches, Colors, No. 00, White Body, Red and Green Decorations. No. 001, Yellow Body, Red, Green and Black Decorations. No. 002, Red Body with Black Decorations.

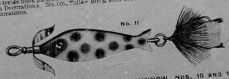

No. 11

HEDDON'S "DOWAGIAC" MINNOW, NOS. 10 AND 11

Has one spinner at head and natural fish tail formation at rear. Weight ¼ ounce, length of body 2¾ inches. Has no side hooks and one single rear hook tied with Bass Fly.

Body portion the new Heddon Hexagon form and beautifully finished in White body with Trouted Spots, No. 10; or Yellow body with Trouted Spots, No. 11.

No. 101 (RAINBOW)

"DOWAGIAC" MINNOW, NO. 100 SERIES

Have two spinners and three extra strong "DOWAGIAC" design nickel plated treble hooks.

Weight, approximately 14 pwts.; length of body 2 3-4 inches. Sink readily.

Furnished in the following variety of beautifully blended colors: No. 100, Fancy Green Back, White Belly; No. 101, Red Body, Dark Green Back; No. 102, White Body with Slate Colored Back; No. 101, Rainbow Colors; No. 109-A, Yellow Perch; No. 109-B, Frog color.

No. 159-A (YELLOW PERCH)

"DOWAGIAC" MINNOW, NO. 150 SERIES

61

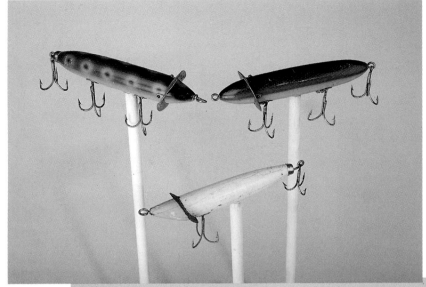

Top left: Dowagiac Surface Lure #200, frog, L-rig, 4 7/8", c.1915-20. $175-250. *Top right:* Dowagiac Surface Lure #200, 2-piece hardware, 4 7/8", c.1930. $100-150. *Bottom:* Dowagiac Perfect Surface Casting Bait, rare yellow head with red collar, 4 1/2", c.1904. $800-1000.

Top left: Dowagiac Surface Lure #200 with box, 2-piece hardware, c.1933. $75-100. *Top right:* Deep-O-Diver #7000 with box, 2 1/2", c.1920. $40-50. *Bottom:* Little Luny Frog #3400, 3 3/4", c.1925. $75-100.

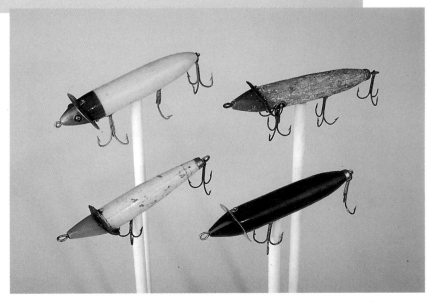

Top left: Dowagiac Surface Lure #200, rare glass eyes, 4 7/8", c.1930. $175-250. *Top right:* Dowagiac Surface Lure #200, Cup-rig, rare four treble hooks, 4 7/8", c.1915. $200-300. *Lower left:* Dowagiac Perfect Surface Casting Bait, 4 1/2", c.1904. $200-300. *Lower right:* Dowagiac Surface Lure #200, unusual solid red, 4 7/8", c.1915. $200-300.

Dowagiac Minnows #210, 3 1/2", c.1920. *Top left:* Unusual red scale. $100-150. *Top right:* Unusual green scale. $100-150. *Lower left:* Early glass eye, most common color, blue & white. $50-75. *Lower right:* Early glass eye, frog. $100-150.

Left: Black Sucker Minnow #1300, Cup-rig, 5 3/4", c.1925. $700-1000. *Right:* Black Sucker Minnow #1300, L-rig, 5 3/4", c.1930. $700-1000.

Dowagiac Minnow #150, special order from factory without hooks, c.1910. *Left:* L-rig hardware, frog pattern. $200-250. *Right:* Cup-rig hardware, rainbow. $200-250.

Far left: Flat-Nose Crab Wiggler #1800, uncataloged, green, 4 1/8", c.1915. $300-400. *Others shown:* Dowagiac Minnow #300, various prop styles and colors, 4", c.1915. $300-400 each.

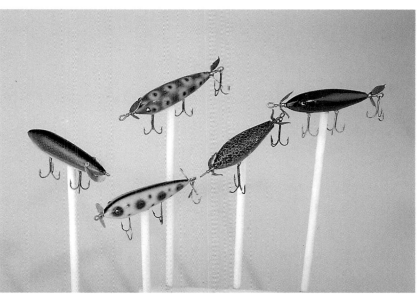

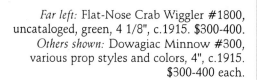

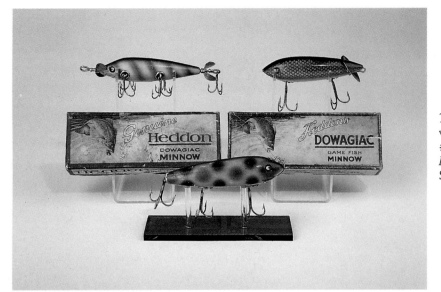

Top left: Dowagiac Minnow #150, Cup-rig, perch, 3 3/4", with box, c.1910. $100-150. *Top right:* Crab Wiggler #1800, green scale, 3 7/8", with box, c.1920. $100-150. *Bottom:* Near Surface Wiggler #1700, carnival, 3", c.1915. $100-150.

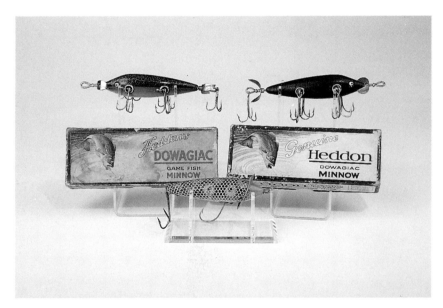

Top left: Dowagiac Minnow #150, Cup-rig, red scale, 3 3/4", with early downward jumping bass box, c.1913. $100-150. *Top right:* Dowagiac Minnow #100, L-rig, red, 2 3/4", c.1918. $75-100. *Bottom:* Dowagiac Minnow #210, L-rig, rare snake skin pattern, 3 1/2", c.1920. $100-150.

Dowagiac Minnow #100, "fat body" style, assorted colors, 2 5/8", c.1917. $100-150.

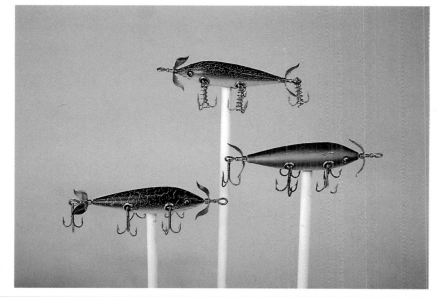

Top: Dowagiac Minnow #150, Cup-rig, 5 weedless treble hooks, green crackle back, 4 1/4", c.1906. $150-200. *Center right:* Dowagiac Minnow #150, Cup-rig, earliest style, rainbow, 4 1/4", c.1906. $150-200. *Lower left:* Dowagiac Minnow #150, L-rig, green crackle back, 4 1/4", c.1920. $100-150.

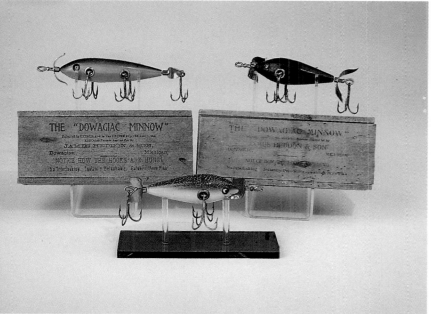

Top left: Dowagiac Minnow #150, orange, Cup-rig, with wooden box, 4 1/4", c.1910. $200-250. *Top right:* Dowagiac Minnow #100, red, Cup-rig, "fat body" style in wooden box, 3 3/4", c.1909. $200-250. *Bottom:* Dowagiac Minnow #100, green crackle back, Cup-rig, "fat body" style. 3 3/4", c.1909. $100-150.

Dowagiac Minnow #150, assorted colors, 2 5/8"- 3", c.1915. $100-200 each.

Dowagiac Minnow #150. 3 3/4"- 4 1/4". *Top left:* Scale, L-rig, c.1918. $100-150. *Lower left:* Red crackle back, Cup-rig, c.1913. $150-200. *Top right:* Perch, L-rig, c.1918. $150-200. *Lower right:* Red & White, Cup-rig, c.1913. $100-125.

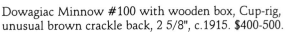

Dowagiac Minnow #100 with wooden box, Cup-rig, unusual brown crackle back, 2 5/8", c.1915. $400-500.

Left to right: Dowagiac Minnow #300, rainbow, 4", c.1910. $150-200; Dowagiac Minnow #300, green crackle back, 4", c.1910. $150-200; Musky Surfusser #300, green crackle back, 3 5/8", c.1930. $150-200; Spin Diver #30000, frog, 4 1/2", c.1918. $250-300; Dowagiac Swimming Minnow #900, carnival, 4 1/2", c.1910. $200-250.

Top left: Artistic Minnow #50, brown crackle back, 1 3/4", c.1907. $100-150. *Lower left:* Multiple Metal Minnow #500, 2 1/2", c.1910. $200-300. *Top right:* Walton Feather Tail #40, 2 3/8", c.1929. $50-75. *Lower right:* River Runt #110, wooden, 2 5/8", c.1930. $20-25.

Top left: Near Surface Wiggler #1700, carnival, 3", c.1915. $75-100. *Lower left:* Musky Surface Minnow #300, carnival, 4", c.1930. $100-150. *Top right:* Surface Minnow #300, red & white, 3 3/4", c.1910. $125-175. *Lower right:* Near Surface Wiggler #1700, rainbow, 3", c.1915. $75-100.

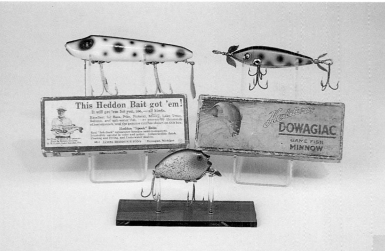

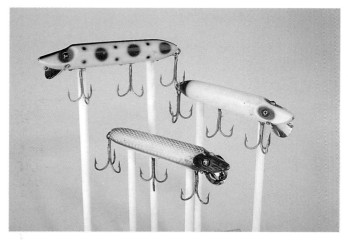

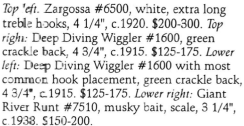

Top left: Flap-tail Musky #7050 with box, carnival, 5 1/4", c.1930. $75-100. *Top right:* Dowagiac Minnow #0, carnival, 3 3/4", c.1915. $150-200. *Bottom:* Punkinseed #740, wooden, 2 1/2", c.1940. $25-35.

Vamp #7500 & Vamp #7300 (jointed), assorted colors, 4 1/2"- 4 3/4", c.1920. $40-50 each.

Top left: Musky vamp #7550, 6", c.1928. $150-200. *Center right and Bottom:* Great Vamp #7540, c.1937. $50-75 each.

Top left: Zaragossa #6500, white, extra long treble hooks, 4 1/4", c.1920. $200-300. *Top right:* Deep Diving Wiggler #1600, green crackle back, 4 3/4", c.1915. $125-175. *Lower left:* Deep Diving Wiggler #1600 with most common hook placement, green crackle back, 4 3/4", c.1915. $125-175. *Lower right:* Giant River Runt #7510, musky bait, scale, 3 1/4", c.1938. $150-200.

Top left: Crab Wiggler #1800, rare red scale, 4", c.1917. $75-100. *Top right:* Dowagiac Minnow #150, Cup-rig, rare white glitter, 3 3/4", c.1915. $200-300. *Bottom:* Dowagiac Minnow #10, carnival, 2 1/2", c.1920. $100-150.

67

Top left: Florida Special #10B, 3 1/2", c.1921. $200-300. *Top right:* Tad Polly #5100, 3", c.1930. $150-200. *Lower left:* Dowagiac Minnow #20, 2 1/4", c.1930. $50-75. *Lower right:* Moonlight Bait Company, Sea Gull, perch, 4", c.1922. $75-100.

Top left: Gamefisher #5500 with box, green scale, 4 1/2", c.1900. $25-35. *Top right:* Dowagiac Minnow #100 with box, Cup-rig, rare snake skin scale, 2 3/4", c.1913. $150-200. *Bottom:* Near Surface Wiggler #1700, early version, green scale, 3", c.1915. $75-100.

Top left: Dowagiac Minnow #00, Cup-rig, red, c.1915. $200-250. *Center left:* Dowagiac Minnow #175, Cup-rig, green crackle back, 3 3/4", c.1910. $200-250. *Top right:* Surface Minny #260, carnival, 3", c.1934. $200-300. *Center:* Dowagiac Minnow #0, Cup-rig, carnival, 3", c.1915. $150-200. *Bottom:* Zaragossa #6500, green scale, 4 1/4", c.1920. $150-200.

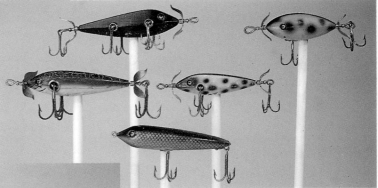

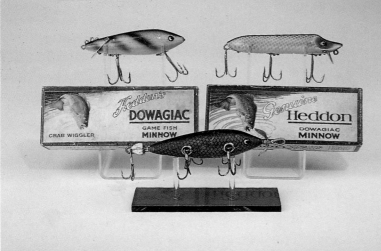

Top left: Crab Wiggler #1800 with box, perch scale, 4", c.1916. $50-75. *Top right:* Vamp #7500 with box, scale, 4 1/2", c.1930. $30-40. *Bottom:* Dowagiac Minnow #150, rare L-rig, green scale, 3 3/4", c.1920. $100-150.

Top left: Jointed Zig-Wag #8300, 3 1/2", c.1935. $35-40. *Center left:* Darting Zara #6600, frog, 3 7/8", c.1930. $100-150. *Top right:* S.O.S.(Swims on Surface), Wounded Minnow #170, perch scale, 4 1/2", c.1925. $50-75. *Center:* Round Nose Vamp, 4 5/8", c.1925. $200-300. *Bottom:* Deep-O-Diver #7000, orange scale, 2 1/2", c.1920. $50-75.

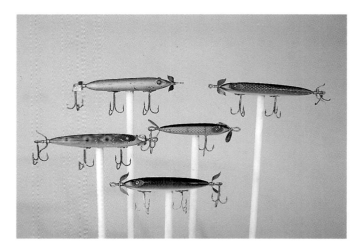

Torpedo #130, various color patterns, 3"- 4", c.1920. $50-75 each.

Top: Tad Polly #5000 in special introductory boxes, 3 5/8", c.1925. $200-250 each. *Bottom:* Baby Crab Wiggler #1900, 3 1/8", c.1916. $25-35.

Top left: Tad Polly #600, red scale, 3 1/4", c.1924. $50-60. *Top right:* Tad Polly #5000, green scale, 3 5/8", c.1925. $50-60. *Lower left:* Tad Polly #5000, snake scale, 3 5/8", c.1925. $50-60. *Lower right:* Crab Wiggler #1800, snake scale, 4", c.1920. $50-75.

Punkinseed #740, wooden, various colors, 2 1/2", c.1940. $25-50 each.

Crazy Crawlers, assorted colors, 2 1/2", c.1940. $25-35 each.

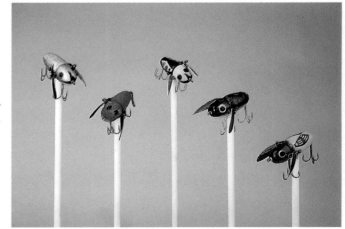

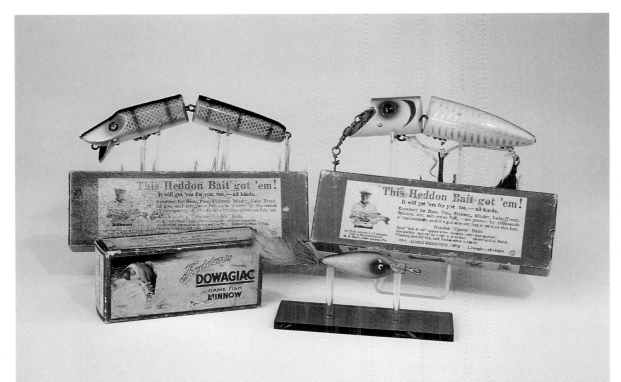

Top left: Jointed
Musky Vamp #7350
with box, 4 7/8",
c.1930. $75-100. *Top
right:* King Zig-Wag
#8350 with box, 5",
c.1930. $40-60.
Bottom: Walton
Feather tail #40 with
box, 2 3/8", c.1920.
$50-75.

Top left: Jointed Vamp #7350, 4 7/8", c.1925. $50-75. *Top right:*
Great Vamp #7540, 5", c.1935. $100-150. *Bottom:* Musky Vamp
#7550, 6", c.1925. $150-175.

Top left: Flap tail #7000, 4", c.1935. $30-50. *Top right:*
Flap tail Musky #7050, mouse, 6 3/4", c.1935. $125-
150. *Center:* Flap tail Musky #7050, 6 3/4", c.1930.
$100-150. *Bottom:* Flap tail Jr. #7110, 2 1/2", c.1930.
$25-35.

Top left: Basser #8500, 4", c.1920. $15-20. *Top right:* Lucky 13 #2500, 3 3/4", c.1940. $20-25. *Lower left:* Wiggler King #2000, 3 3/4", c.1920. $30-40. *Lower right:* Head-on Basser #8540, 4 1/2", c.1922. $15-20.

Heddon "spook" lures are made of "Heddylin" plastic. *Top left:* Torpedo, 4", c.1930. $25-30. *Lower left:* Vamp, 4". $35-40. *Top right:* Sea Runt #610 with box, 2 5/8", c.1937. $25-35. *Lower right:* Common River Runt, 2 1/2", c.1940. $10-15 .

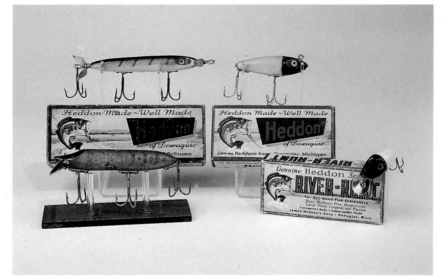

Sonar Lure in store display carton, 2" metal bait, c.1940. $10-15 each.

Ernest F. Pflueger, Akron, Ohio had patented his soft rubber minnows which were used for the company's spearing decoys and casting baits in 1892, years before Heddon commercially manufactured its first fishing lure in 1898. Pflueger established himself in the tackle business when he started the American Fish Hook Company based in his home town, Akron, Ohio in 1864. His tackle company continued to exist in the Pflueger family hands as the Akron Fishing Tackle Works, the Enterprise Manufacturing Company and finally the Pflueger Tackle Company. Although the company concentrated heavily on reels and metal baits, Pflueger was fascinated by the use of the newly developed luminous paints which he utilized on soft rubber and cedar baits creating the family's fishing tackle empire. One of the company's earliest patents was for a molded soft rubber minnow invented by Adrian Holbrook. Details like eyes, gill, scales and an open mouth were molded directly into the fish.

73

Pflueger Musky Never Fail Minnow, 5", c.1910. $800-1000.

Pflueger Never Fail Minnow #3100, assorted colors, 3"- 3 5/8", c.1907. $75-100 each.

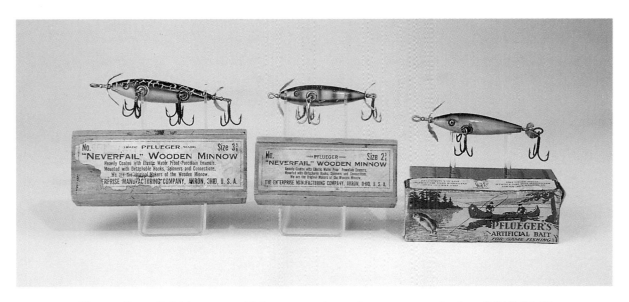

Pflueger Never Fail Minnows with boxes, wooden and paper, assorted colors, 2 3/4"-3 1/4", c.1907. $100-150 each.

Top: Pflueger Mustang, 2 3/4", c.1930. $20-25. *Bottom:* Pflueger Surprise Minnow, 3 1/4", c.1920. $100-125.

The history of the PawPaw Company is closely tied into that of the Moonlight Bait Company started in 1906 by Horace Ball and Charles Varney of Paw Paw, Michigan who advocated night fishing using luminous baits. For years they operated their bait business from the basement of Paw Paw City Hall where Ball was the janitor. The bait blanks were turned elsewhere then finished, assembled and painted at the courthouse. In 1927, Moonlight employees Floyd Phelps and Clyde Sinclair patented a silver flashing feature. By this time, the Moonlight Bait Company had began the transition into the Paw Paw Bait Company which was incorporated in 1935 with Sinclair as the president.

Top left: Moonlight Bait Company Floating Bait #1, 4", c.1910. $25-50. *Top right:* T.J. Boulton, Detroit, Michigan, Bass Hog, 3 3/8", c.1910. $100-150. *Bottom:* Moonlight Bait Company Floating Bait #1, first production bait, 4 3/8", c.1909. $25-50.

Moonlight Bait Company. *Top left:* Jointed Pikaroon #2000, 4 1/2", c.1928. $75-100. *Lower left:* Musky Pikaroon, 5 1/4", c.1926. $100-125. *Top right:* Pikaroon #1000, 4 1/4", c.1922. $75-100. *Lower right:* Single Hook Pikaroon #2500, 4 1/4", c.1923. $75-100.

Moonlight Bait Company. *Top left:* Torpedo #2900, 4", c.1926. $50-75. *Lower left:* Pikaroon #900, 4 1/4", c.1923. $75-100. *Top right:* Moonlight #3354, 3 1/2", c.1925. $35-50. *Lower right:* Underwater Minnow, 3 1/2", c.1928. $75-100.

Paw Paw Bait Company. *Top left and right:* Jointed Trout Caster, 3 5/8", c.1935. $25-30 each. *Lower left:* Jointed Trout Minnow, 4", c.1920. $50-75. *Lower right:* Trout Caster, 3 1/2", c.1930. $25-30.

Top left: Moonlight Bait Company Floating Bait #1, 4 3/8", c.1910. $25-50. *Top right:* South Bend Tackle Company Woodpecker Bait #923, 4 3/4", c.1919. $35-50. *Bottom:* South Bend Tackle Company Weedless Midget Woodpecker #926, 3", c.1920. $75-100.

The South Bend Bait Company evolve out of a small bait company started by F.G. Worden, inventor of the bucktail bait in 1896. With new investment capital from Chicago and the employment of Ivar Hennings, an avid angler and soon company president, South Bend became one of the major suppliers of commercial fishing tackle, distributing throughout the United States, Canada and France by 1917.

William Shakespeare Jr., Kalamazoo, Michigan established his tackle company by the same name during the late 1890s. His first patent was awarded for a level wind reel in 1892 and by February of 1901 he had a patent for the wooden model of the Revolution bait. This was the first of an impressive line of fishing baits which Shakespeare built by acquiring additional patent rights from other tackle makers like Jay B. Rhodes. Rhodes who also lived in Kalamazoo, Michigan produced a small line of handmade fishing plugs with his uncle Fred D. Rhodes and Bert O. Rhodes under the Kalamazoo Fishing Tackle Company including the Rhodes Wooden Minnow with see-through hardware and the Rhodes mechanical frog. After William Shakespeare died in 1950, his company was sold to the Creek Chub Bait Company (1952).

Worden Bucktail Bait Company (South Bend Bait Company). *Top left:* Uncataloged bait, 3", c.1900. $300-400. *Top right:* Uncataloged bait, 3 1/4", c.1900. $300-400. *Lower left:* uncataloged bait with bucktail, 2 3/4", c.1900. $300-400. *Lower right:* Pflueger Peerless Minnow, 2 1/2", c.1912. $50-75.

Most of the major
tackle companies used production
lines such as these at Gladding Corporation, Garret,
Indiana, where lures were produced under the well-
known name, the South Bend Bait Company, c.1940.
Photo courtesy of Dan Basore's Historical Fishing Display.

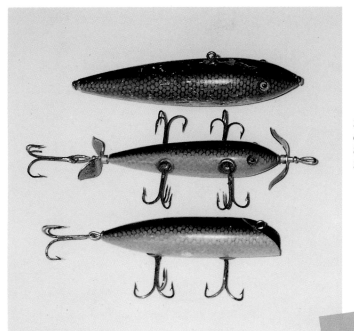

South Bend Bait Company. *Top:* Ice spearing decoy, green scale, 5 1/4", c.1924. $400-600. *Center:* Underwater Minnow #905, green scale, 3 5/8", c.1915. $100-125. *Bottom:* Bass-Oreno, green scale, 3 1/2", c.1916. $25-50. *Photo courtesy of Frank Baron.*

Top left: Underwater Minnow #905, 3", c.1915. $100-125. *Lower left:* Worden/South Bend Minnow #931 (buck tail missing), 3", c.1920. $40-50. *Top right:* Surface Minnow, 3 1/2", c.1910. $100-125. *Lower right:* Underwater Minnow #905, 3", c.1915. $100-125.

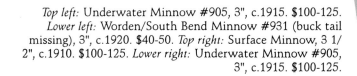

South Bend Minnows. *Top left:* Surface Minnow #921, 3 1/2", c.1910. $100-150. *Top right:* Three Treble Underwater Minnow #903, 3", c.1910. $100-150. *Lower left:* Panetella Minnow #913, 4 1/4", c.1920. $35-50. *Lower right:* Panetella Minnow #913 with early brass cap, 4 1/4", c.1912. $50-75.

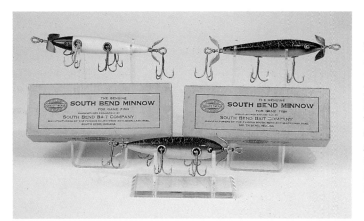

Top left: Panetella #915 with box, 4 1/4", c.1920. $50-75. *Top right:* Panetella #913 with box, 4 1/4", c.1920. $50-75. *Bottom:* Underwater Minnow #905, 3 5/8", c.1930. $50-75.

Top left: Salt Water Bass-Oreno #977 with box, 3 3/4", c.1930. $35-40. *Top right:* Bass-Oreno #973 with box, 3 1/2", c.1930. $25-35. *Bottom:* Panetella #913, 4 1/2", c.1920. $50-75.

Tarp-Oreno #979, 8", c.1920. $50-75.

Vacuum Bait #21 with box, 2", c.1925. $100-150.

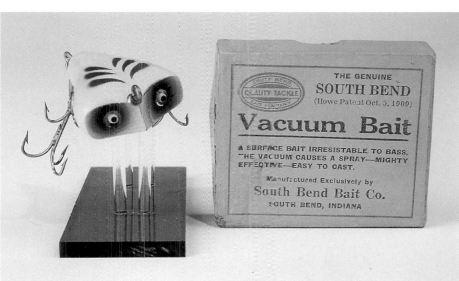

THE GENUINE
SOUTH BEND
(Howe Patent Oct. 5, 1909)
Vacuum Bait
A SURFACE BAIT IRRESISTABLE TO BASS. THE VACUUM CAUSES A SPRAY—MIGHTY EFFECTIVE—EASY TO CAST.
Manufactured Exclusively by
South Bend Bait Co.
SOUTH BEND, INDIANA

Started by George Schuktress, Carl Heinzerling, and Henry S. Dills, the Creek Chub Bait Company shipped its first commercial lure, a #100 wiggler, in 1911 which makes this company a relative late-comer in the fishing tackle market. They were, however, able to gain a strong footing by developing the first natural scale finish for artificial lures which they licensed to the other tackle companies. Creek Chub offers the collector a varied assortment of lures ranging from the highly recognizable "Pikie" baits to the novel beetle and waterbug baits.

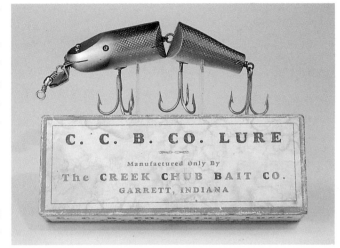

Creek Chub Bait Company, Jointed Husky Pikie #3000 with box, rare blue color, 5 1/4", c.1926. $75-100.

Left, top and Bottom: Tiny Tim #6400, 1 3/4", c.1940. $35-50 each. *Top right:* Baby Beetle, 2", c.1930. $50-60. *Lower right:* Ding Bat #5100, 2", c.1930. $25-30.

Assorted Creek Chub Beetles #3800, 2 1/2", c.1930-1951. $50-75 each.

Left to right: Weed Bug #2800, 2", c.1920. $100-150; Weed Bug #2800, 2", c.1920. $100-150; Weedee #4800, 2 1/2", c.1935. $200-250; Surface Ding Bat #5400, 1 1/4", c.1935. $35-45; Ding Bat #5100, 2", c.1935. $25-35.

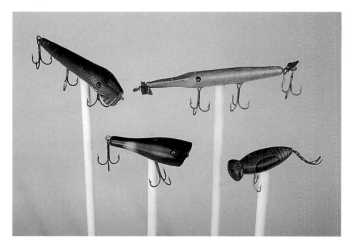

Top left: Sucker, 3 1/2", c.1932. $100-150. *Lower left:* Plunker #3200, 3", c.1925. $40-50; *Top right:* Gar Underwater Minnow #2900, 5 1/4", c.1925. $200-250; *Lower right:* Big Creek Bug Wiggler #1400, 2 1/2", c.1920. $75-100.

Top left: Injured Minnow #1500, 3 1/4", c.1920. Unusual color pattern: $50-75. Common color pattern: $25-30. *Lower left:* Jigger #4100, 3 1/4", c.1930. $75-100. *Top right:* Wiggler #100, 3 1/2", c.1910. $50-75. *Lower right:* Lucky Mouse #3600, 2 1/2", c.1930. $40-60.

Creek Chub Musky Baits. *Top left:* Husky Plunker #5800, 4 1/2", c.1939. $75-100. *Top right:* Jointed Pikie Minnow #2600, 4 1/2", c.1926. $75-100. *Bottom:* Husky Musky Minnow #600 with box, 5", c.1930. $75-100.

Top left: Wiggler #100 with introductory box, 3 1/2", c.1910. $200-300. *Top right:* Open Mouth Shiner #500, 3 1/4", c.1920. $50-75. *Bottom:* Weed Bug #2800, 2", c.1925. $100-150.

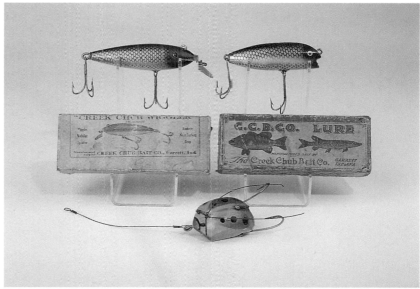

Left: Lauby Bait Company, Marshfield, Wisconsin, Weedless Lauby Bait with box, 4", c.1935. $100-125. *Right:* Shur-Strike Minnow with box, trade lure made by Creek Chub for wholesalers, 3 1/2", c.1930. $25-35.

Not all the collectible lures were produced by the larger tackle companies just mentioned. Several smaller companies like the William Jamison Company, Chicago, Illinois; Fred Keeling and Company, Rockford, Illinois; Wilson (Hastings Sporting Goods Company), Hastings, Michigan; and the J.K. Rush (Union Specialty Company), Syracuse, New York are considered among the top ten collectible lure producers.

Companies like the Winchester Repeating Arms Company, New Haven, Connecticut made their presence known in the fishing tackle market by distributing tackle made by other manufacturers under their label. This practice is known as a "trade" lure. In the case of Winchester lures, this in no way detracts from the value of the lure. There are other trade lures that are also considered good collectibles. Small tackle companies, sometimes run out of a basement or garage, have also produced a quality line of collectible lures as have certain individuals. All these producers made up an important part of fishing paraphernalia collecting.

84

Amid the fierce competition for the fishermen business, companies used any means to get the word out about their latest innovations. During the 1920s the William Shakespeare Company gave these hard rubber display boards to their dealers. $75-100.

Top left: Revolution, 3 1/2",
c.1909. $75-100. *Lower left:*
Worden Bucktail Revolution, 2",
c.1902. $100-125. *Top right:*
Musky Revolution, 4 1/4",
c.1902. $250-300. *Lower right:*
Worden Bucktail Revolution, 2
1/4", c.1910. $75-100.

Submerged Wooden Minnow
#44, assorted colors with early
wooden and paper boxes, 3 3/4",
c.1910. $175-200 each.

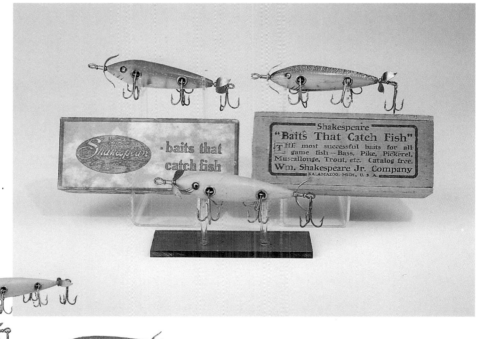

Assorted Wooden Minnows by Wm.
Shakespeare Bait Company, 3"-5",
c.1908-1915. Five hooks: $300-500
each. Three hooks: $200-300 each.

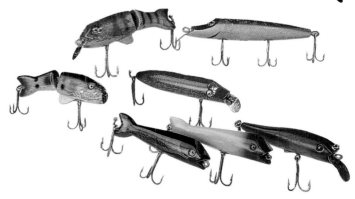

85

Top left: Strike-It #666, 3 3/4", c.1930. $75-100. *Center left:* Tantalizer
#638, 4", c.1930. $50-75. *Top right:* Pikie Kazoo #637, 4 1/2", c.1925.
$75-100. *Center:* Kazoo Wobbler #6637, 4", c.1925. $75-100. *Lower left
and center:* Plopper #6511, 3 3/4", c.1927. $50-75 each. *Lower right:*
Kazoo Chub Minnow, 3 5/8", c.1925. $75-100.

W.J. Jamison Factory, 2751 Polk Street, Chicago, Illinois, c.1906. The basis of the Jamison production line was the Coaxer as seen worn by these ladies as a pin. When William Jamison died in 1926, he had been responsible for originating 22 bait casting lures, 18 fly lures, and 7 fishing hooks. The company continued to produce baits and spinners by various relatives until it was sold in 1952. *Photo Courtesy of Dan Basore's Historical Fishing Display.*

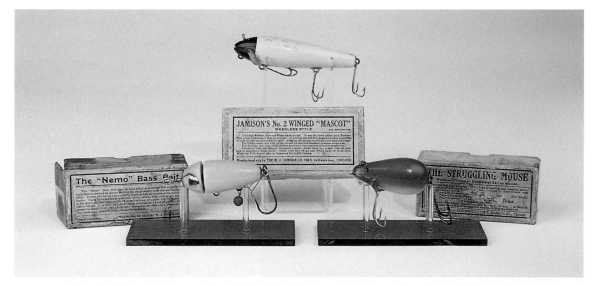

Top: #1 Winged Mascot, 4", c.1915. $75-100. *Lower left:* Nemo Bass Bait, 2 3/8", c.1910. $200-300. *Lower right:* Struggling Mouse, 2 1/4", c.1915. $75-100.

Top left: Clark Expert, J.L. Clark Manufacturing Company, Rockford, Illinois, 2 1/2", c.1905. $200-300. *Top right:* Charmer Minnow, Charmer Minnow Company, Springfield, Missouri, 3 3/8", c.1910. $200-300. *Lower left:* Clark Expert, 3", c.1905. $200-300. *Lower right:* Clark Expert, early no eyes, 3", c.1905. $200-300.

Fred C. Keeling bought the rights to the J.L. Clark Manufacturing Company in 1814. *Top left:* Pike Kee-Wig, 4 1/2", c.1925. $75-100. *Top right:* Baby Pike Kee-Wig, 3 1/2", c.1928. $75-100. *Center:* Musky Crawfish, 3 3/4", c.1925. $50-75. *Lower left:* Pike Kee-Wig, 4 1/2", c.1925. $65-100. *Lower right:* Surface Tom, 3 1/4", c.1920. $40-50.

The novel Chippewa bait was produced by the Immell Bait Company, Blair, Wisconsin, c.1915. *Top left:* Musky Chippewa Bait, 5", c.1913. $300-400. *Others shown:* Various colors and sizes, 3"- 4", c.1913. $200-300 each.

Probably the most collectible of the "trade lure" (A trade lure was manufactured to be sold by a distributor.) were sold under the name of the Winchester Repeating Arms Company, New Haven, Connecticut, c.1921. *Top left:* 5 Hook Winchester Minnow with box, 4". $750-100. *Top right:* Multi-Wobbler with box, 3 1/2", $500-750. *Bottom:* 3 Hook Winchester Minnow, 3 1/4". $500-600.

Assorted Winchester Repeating Arms Company 5 Hook Minnows and 3 Hook Minnows, 3 1/4"- 4", c.1921. $500-700 each.

Assorted Winchester Repeating Arms Company Multi-Wobbler, 3 1/2", c.1921. $300-400 each.

Top left: Metal Weedless Bait, Rubin Danielson, Chicago, Illinois, 4 1/4", patent 1927. $250-300. *Lower left:* Unknown, 2 3/4", possible South Bend Bait Company Prototype, c.1920. $75-100. *Top right:* Spoon Fish, General Tool Company, Minnesota, 2 3/4", c.1930. $150-200. *Lower right:* King Wiggler, King Bait Company, Minnesota, 3 1/2", c.1915. $50-75.

Top left: Waukazoo Surface Spinner #6555, Wm. Shakespeare Company, 2 1/2", c.1930. $50-75. *Center left:* Weller's Classic Minnow, Erwin Weller Company, Sioux City, Iowa, 3 1/2", c.1920. $75-100. *Bottom:* Whirl-Oreno #955, South Bend Bait Company, 3", c.1930. $75-100. *Center:* Wilson Grass Widow, Hastings Sporting Goods Works, Michigan, 2 1/4", c.1920. $75-100. *Top right:* Getsem Weedless Bait, patented by F.L. Algers, Grand Rapids, Michigan, Hastings Sporting Goods Works, Michigan, 2 1/4", c.1915. $250-300.

Top left: Schoonie's Skooter, J.R. Schoonmaker, Michigan, 4", c.1916. $100-150. *Top right:* Unknown, 3", c.1900. $75-100. *Lower left:* Eureka Wiggler, Eureka Bait Company, Coldwater, Michigan, 4 1/4", c.1915. $15-200. *Lower right:* Coldwater Ghost, Coldwater Bait Company, Michigan, 4", c.1915. $150-200.

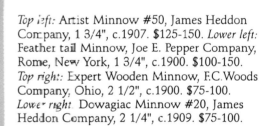

Top left: Artist Minnow #50, James Heddon Company, 1 3/4", c.1907. $125-150. *Lower left:* Feather tail Minnow, Joe E. Pepper Company, Rome, New York, 1 3/4", c.1900. $100-150. *Top right:* Expert Wooden Minnow, F.C. Woods Company, Ohio, 2 1/2", c.1900. $75-100. *Lower right:* Dowagiac Minnow #20, James Heddon Company, 2 1/4", c.1909. $75-100.

Top right: O'Boy Minnow, Pflueger Bait Company, 3 1/2", c.1920. $40-60. *Top left:* Strike Killer, 3 3/4", c.1930. $100-150. *Lower left:* Rush Tiger Tango, J.K. Rush (Union Specialty Company), Syracuse, New York, 4", c.1920. $75-90. *Lower right:* Unknown surface bait, 2 1/2", c.1900. $50-75.

89

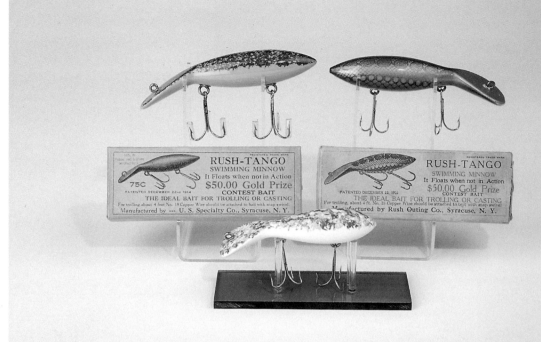

Top: Tango with boxes, J.K. Rush Company, 5", c.1915. $100-150 each. *Bottom:* Tango Jr., 4", c.1918. $100-150.

Top left: Panetella Minnow, South Bend Bait Company, 4 1/4", c.1920. $75-100. *Lower left:* Uncataloged South Bend Bait Company, 4 1/4", c.1910. $75-100. *Top right:* Ozark Wiggler, Erwin Weller Company, Sioux City, Iowa, 3", c.1930. $50-75. *Lower right:* Frog Skin Bait, Wm. Shakespeare Company, 3 1/4", c.1930. $50-75.

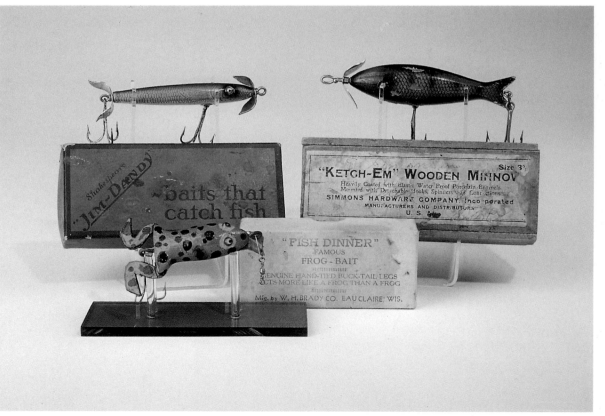

Top left: Jim Dandy Torpedo with box, Wm. Shakespeare Company, c.1930. $50-75. *Top right:* Ketch-Em Wooden Minnow with box, Simmons Hardware Store, 3 1/2", c.1920. $75-150. *Bottom:* Fish Dinner Frog Bait with box, W.H. Brady Company, 2 5/8", c.1920. $200-300.

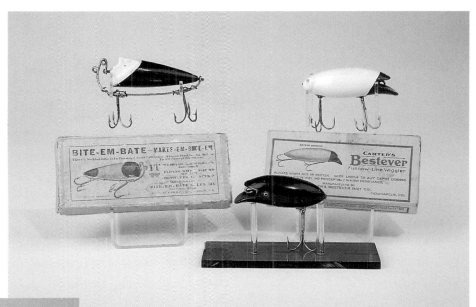

Top left: Bite-Em-Bate with box, Bite-Em-Bate Company (pre-1920 spelling), Warsaw, Indiana, 2 7/8", c.1917. $50-75. *Top right:* Carter's Midget Bestever #10 with box, Carter's Bestever Bait Company, Indianapolis, Indiana, 2 7/8", c.1925. $40-50. *Bottom:* Carter's Midget Bestever #10 with glass eyes, 2 7/8", c.1930. $40-50.

Top left to right: Water Puppy, Barr-Royers Company, Waterloo, Iowa, 2", c.1920. $75-100; Tin Liz Sunfish, glass eyes, Fred Arbogast Baits, Akron, Ohio, 1 1/2", c.1930. $400-500; Craw Dad's Flapper Crab, Wright & McGill Company, Denver, Colorado, 2 1/2", c.1930. $75-100. *Lower left:* Craw Dad's Flapper Crab, Wright & McGill Company, 1 3/4", c.1930. $75-100. *Lower right:* Tin Liz Sunfish, glass eyes, Fred Arbogast Baits, 2", c.1930. $400-500.

Top left: Johnson Automatic Striker, Carl A Johnson, Chicago, Illinois, 2", c.1935. $50-75. *Top right:* Crippled Wiggler, signed, Bud Stewart, Flint, Michigan, 2 1/2", c.1930. $150-200. *Center:* Magnifying Glass Minnow Tube, Detroit Glass Minnow Company, 3 1/4", c.1915. $300-400. *Bottom:* Darters, Louis Rhead, New York, 3"-5", c.1910. $100-150.

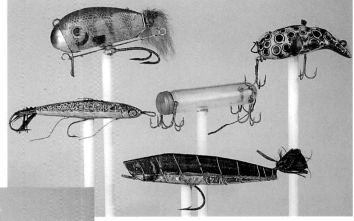

91

Left: Moonlight #3354 with box, Moonlight Bait Company & Novelty Works, Michigan, 3 1/2", c.1925. $75-100. *Right:* Sterling Wooden Minnow with box, 3 1/2", c.1900. $200-300.

Left: Muskegon Spoon Jack Minnow, 4 1/4", c.1920. $200-250. *Right:* Bassy Getum #1200 with box, Outing Manufacturing Company, Indiana, 3 7/8", c.1930. $75-100.

Top left: Unknown bait, 3 1/2", c.1910. $50-75. *Top Right:* Zig-Zag Jr., 2 1/2", c.1914. $40-50. *Lower left:* Water Puppy, Barr-Royer, Waterloo, Iowa, 4", c.1931. $50-75. *Lower right:* Paw Paw Bullhead #3500, Paw Paw Bait Company, 4 1/4", c.1931. $100-150.

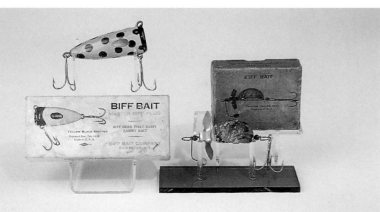

Biff Bait Company, Milwaukee, Wisconsin. *Left:* Master Biff Plug, water sonic style with box, 2 1/2", c.1925. $50-75. *Right:* Surface Single Wobbler, 2", c.1925. $60-75.

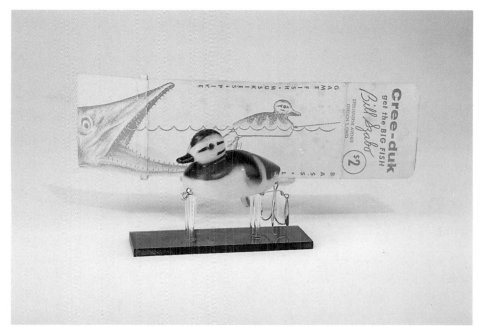

Cree-Duk (musky bait), Bill Szabo, 2 1/2", c.1940. $50-75.

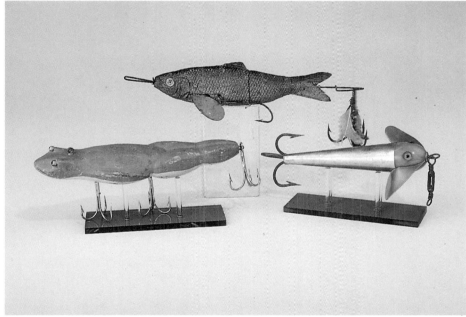

Musky Baits. *Top:* Muskallonge, Pflueger, Akron, Ohio, 7", c.1890. $700-800. *Lower left:* Swimming frog, handmade, unknown maker, northern Minnesota, 9", c.1920. $400-500. *Lower right:* Unknown English phantom type bait, Bakelite and metal, 5", c.1910. $75-100.

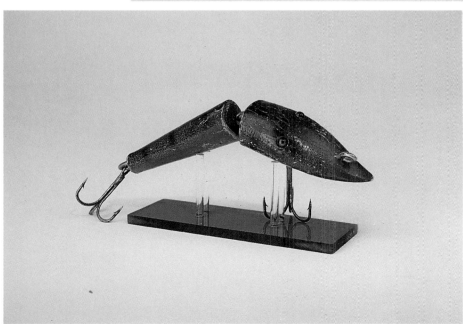

Musky Pikaroon, Moonlight Bait Company, 5 1/2", c.1920. $200-300.

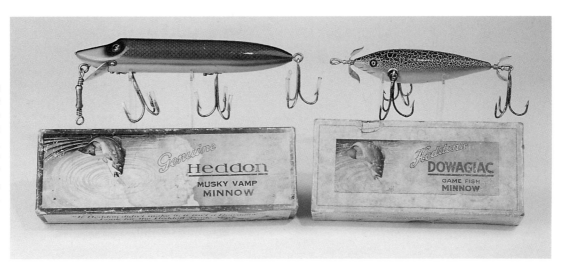

James Heddon & Sons Tackle Company musky baits. *Left:* Musky Vamp #7600 with box, 8", c.1920. $200-300. *Right:* Muskollonge Minnow #700 with box, 5", c.1910. $400-500.

James Heddon & Sons Tackle Company's musky baits. *Top left:* Coast Minnow #4, carnival, 5", c.1915. $300-400. *Top right:* Musky Surfusser # 300, six hook, 5 3/8", c.1930. $225-275. *Lower left:* Musky Surfusser #300, 5 3/8", c.1930. $175-200. *Lower right:* Musky Crazy Crawler #2150, 3 1/2", c.1940. $45-50.

Top: Musky Minnow #64, Wm. Shakespeare Company, 5 1/4", c.1918. $350-400. *Bottom:* Muskollonge Minnow #700, James Heddon & Sons Tackle Company, Cup-rig, 5", c.1911. $400-500 each.

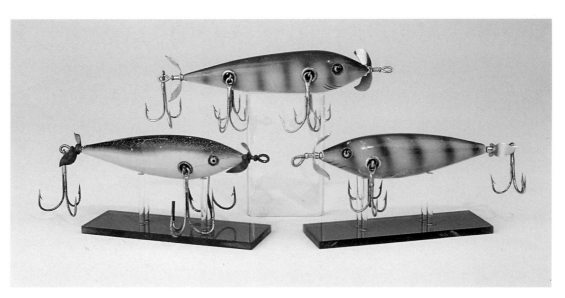

Close-ups from center photo:
Top left to right: Lunge-Oreno #966, South Bend Bait Company, 5 3/4", c.1930. $125-150; Husky Injured Minnow #3500, Creek Chub Bait Company, 5", c.1930. $50-75; Husky Musky #600, Creek Chub Bait Company, 5", c.1920. $75-100.

Left to right: Surfster #7300, Creek Chub Bait Company, 6", c.1950 $40-50; Lunge-Oreno #966, South Bend Bait Company, c.1920. $125-150; Husky Injured Minnow #3500, Creek Chub Bait Company, 5", c.1930. $50-75; Husky Musky #600, Creek Chub Bait Company, 5", c.1920. $75-100.

Close-up from center photo: Creek Chub Bait Company Surfster #7300, 6", c.1950. $40-50.

Master Muskie Wiggler with box, 3 1/2", c.1930. $50-75.

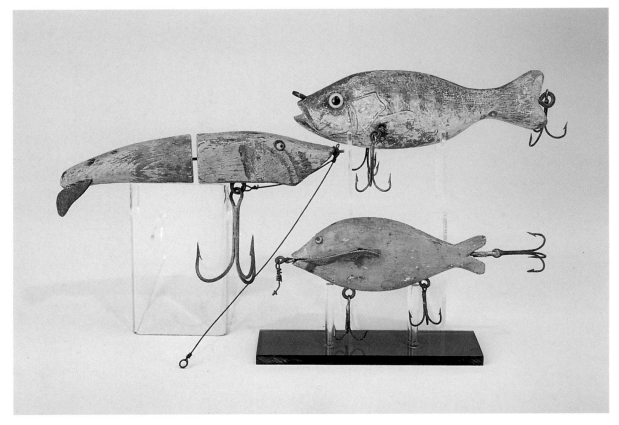

Handmade unknown musky baits. *Top:* Perch, 6", c.1940. $150-200. *Center left:* Jointed copy of Mud Puppy, 6 1/2", c.1940. $75-100. *Bottom:* Yellow sunfish with copper fins, 5", c.1930. $100-150.

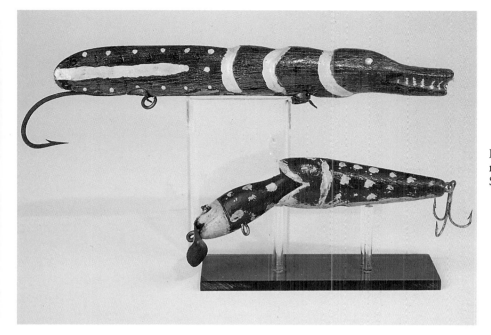

Folksy unknown musky baits from northern Minnesota, 6"- 9", c.1940. $75-100 each.

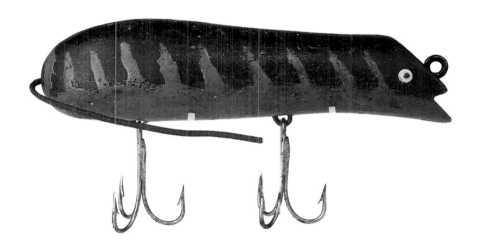

Homemade copy of Shakespeare swimming mouse used for musky, 6", c.1940. $75-100.

97

Miscellaneous handmade lures with decorated tackle box, unknown Minnesota maker. $75-100 each. Box: $50.

Assortment of handmade crawfish and frogs from northern Minnesota, makers unknown, c.1930. $75-100 each.

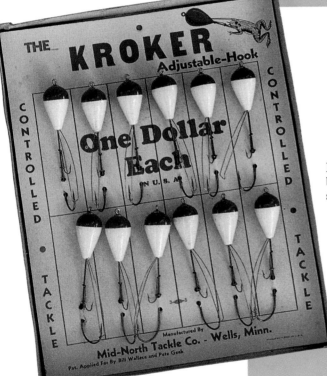

Fishermen have long considered live frogs to be excellent bait. Devices like this Kroker adjustable hook were specially made to hold live frogs, c.1950. $40-50.

For whatever reason, some fishermen just preferred to make their own baits. *Left to right:* Frog bait, maker unknown, 4", c.1930. $75-100; Hollow wooden mouse with copper bottom plate and leather tail, maker unknown, Wisconsin, 3 1/2", c.1920. $200-300; Mechanical lake trout lure, spring-loaded hooks, Fred Lexow, Balsam Lake, Minnesota, c.1935. $150-200; Duckling musky bait, unknown Minnesota maker, c.1930. $100-150; Multi-jointed crawfish, maker unknown, 5 1/2", c.1920. $75-100.

The natural form of the frog inspired countless interesting lures. Gee-Wiz Bait Company frog lure on card, 4', c.1938. $100-150.

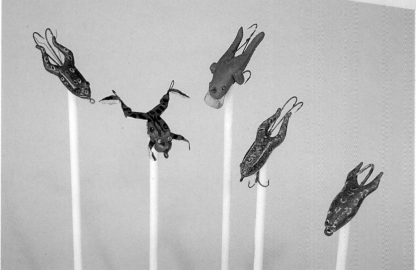

Left to right: Soft Rubber Frog, Pfleuger Bait Company, Akron, Ohio, 2 7/8", c.1905. $75-100; Oscar the Frog, T.F. Auclaire, Michigan, 4 7/8", c.1900. $400-500; Handmade frog, maker unknown, 4", c.1920. $75-100; Floating Meadow Frog, Pfleuger Bait Company, 2 1/2", c.1900. $100-125; Handmade frog, maker unknown, 3", c.1930. $75-100.

Left to right: Floating Meadow Frog, Pfleuger Bait Company, 2 1/2", c.1900. $100-125; Rhodes Mechanical Swimming Frog #3GWF, Wm. Shakespeare Bait Company, 3 1/4", c.1910. $150-200; Hastings Rubber Frog, James J. Hastings, Chicago, Illinois, 3 1/2", c.1895. $150-200; Soft Rubber Frog, Pfleuger Bait Company, 2 7/8", c.1905. $100-125; Floating Meadow Frog, Pfleuger Bait Company, 2 1/2", c.1900. $100-125.

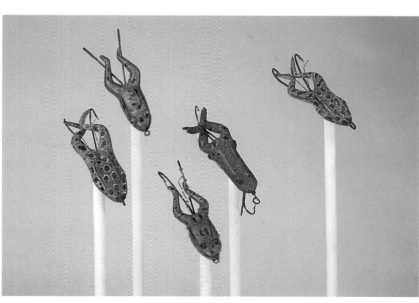
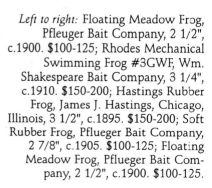

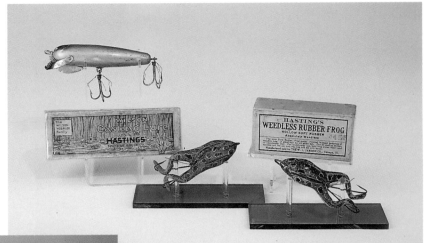

Top left: 6-1 Wobbler with box, Hastings Sporting Goods Works, Hastings, Michigan, 4", c.1917. $150-200. *Lower left:* Floating Meadow Frog, Pflueger Bait Company, 2 7/8", c.1905. $100-125. *Lower right:* Weedless Rubber Frog with box, 3 1/2", c.1890. $150-200.

Left to right: New Weighted Nature Frog, Louis Rhead, Amityville, New York, 3 1/2", c.1920. $400-500; Open Mouth Frog, Wright & McGill Company, 3", c.1925. $150-200; Viking Frog, Viking Bait & Novelty Company, St. Paul. Minnesota, 3 1/2", c.1030. $400-500; Wotta Frog #73, Paw Paw Bait Company, 3 1/2", c.1940. $25-35; Wilson Frog (Stamped "patent 1-8-35"), New York, 2 1/2". $200-300.

Top left: Halik Frog with box & Halik Frog Jr. in box, Halik Company, Moose lake, Minnesota, c.1940. $50-75 each. *Top right:* Froglegs Surface Frog, Jenson Distributing Company, Waco, Texas, c.1940. $75-85. *Lower right:* Froglegs Mechanical Frog, Jenson Distributing Company. $80-100.

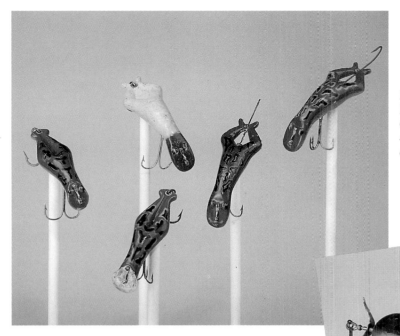

Luny Frogs by James Heddon Company. *Left:* Little Luny #3400, closed legs, 3 1/4", c.1927. $75-100. *Center:* Luny Frog #3500, closed legs, rare red & white, 4 1/4", c.1930. $300-400. *Right:* Luny Frog #3500, early open leg design, c.1927. $75-100.

Assorted Kent Frogs, F.A. Pardee Company, Kent, Ohio, 2 1/2", c.1910-1925. $150-200 each.

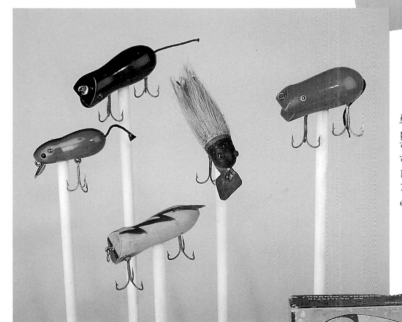

Left to right: Paw Paw Minnie, Paw Paw Bait Company, 2 1/4", c.1930. $25-35; Swimming Mouse Jr., Wm. Shakespeare Company, 2 3/4", c.1930. $25-35; Wizard Wiggler, Pflueger, 3 1/2", c.1920. $40-50; Unknown handmade "hair" mouse, 3", c.1920. $50-75; Swimming Mouse, Shakespeare Company, 2 3/4", c.1930. $25-35.

Most tackle companies offered some type of mouse lure. Inserted dried blood would slowly seep from this "Bleeder" Mouse Bait produced by Bleeding Bait Manufacturing Company, Texas, 2 5/8", c.1930. $100-150.

Left to right: Hair mouse, unknown maker, 2 1/4", c.1920. $25-50; Mouse-Oreno, South Bend Bait Company, 2 3/4", c.1930. $45-50; Minnie Mouse, Paw Paw Bait Company, 2 1/2", c.1930. $45-50; Mouse-Oreno 3949, South Bend Bait Company, 2 3/4", c.1930. $45-50; Meadow Mouse #4000, James Heddon Tackle Company, 2 3/4", c.1920. $35-40.

Left to right: Minnie Mouse, Paw Paw Bait Company, flocked, 2 1/2", c.1930. $25-35; Paw Paw Mouse #50, Moonlight Bait Company, 2 1/2", c.1920. $50-75; The Mouse Bait, Mouse Bait Company, Fort Worth, Texas, 2 1/4", c.1925. $75-100; Minnie Mouse, Paw Paw Bait Company, 2 1/2", c.1930. $25-35; Musky Padler #6679, Wm. Shakespeare Bait Company, 3 3/4", c.1935. $100-125.

Crawfish are also a popular live bait which tackle makers tried to imitate. *Top left:* Midget Tango, Rush Tango Bait Company, 2 1/2", c.1920. $40-50. *Top right:* Crab Spook, James Heddon & Sons Tackle Company, plastic, 2", c.1950. $25-35. *Center:* Baby Crab Wiggler #1900, James Heddon & Sons Tackle Company, 3 1/8", c.1915. $75-100. *Bottom:* Medley's Wiggly Crawfish, F.B. Hamilton Manufacturing, Pasadena, California, 3", c.1920. $150-200.

Various feather popper fly baits. $10-20 each.

Many of the major lure manufacturers offered miniature versions of their casting lure for the fly fisherman. The fly baits shown here barely scratch the surface of still another intriguing realm of collecting.

Assorted feather popper fly baits. *Lower right:* Deer hair was a popular fly tying material often formed into tiny mice.

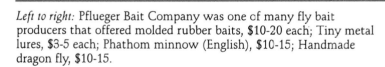

Left to right: Pflueger Bait Company was one of many fly bait producers that offered molded rubber baits, $10-20 each; Tiny metal lures, $3-5 each; Phathom minnow (English), $10-15; Handmade dragon fly, $10-15.

Top left: Pflueger rubber minnows, $15-20 each. *Center left:* Creek Chub Ding Bat Fly baits, $20-30 each. *Lower right:* South Bend Bait Company, $10-15 each. *Top right:* Flat Fish fly baits, $3-5 each.

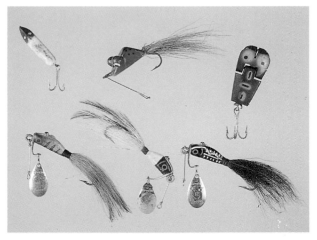

James Heddon & Sons Tackle Company Fly Baits. $15-20 each.

103

Stenciled live bait tin was made to be worn on a belt, $50-75. Assorted Creek Chub and Heddon fly baits, $15-20 each.

Typical deer hair bait which was popular among fishermen. Made by Bill Johnson, this is obviously a mouse, not a "Froggie", 1 1/2", c.1920. $50-75.

Although the wooden lure dominated the tackle market, metal spoon baits were still favored by some fishermen. One of the early metal spoon baits was produced by A.F. Bingenheider, Milwaukee, Wisconsin, Bing's Metal spoons, 2"- 3 1/2", c.1890. $25 each.

Metal baits that are still attached to their original cards are more valuable, especially if the card has good graphics. Bucktail Spinner, Pflueger Bait Company, 3 1/2" spoon, c.1890. $150.

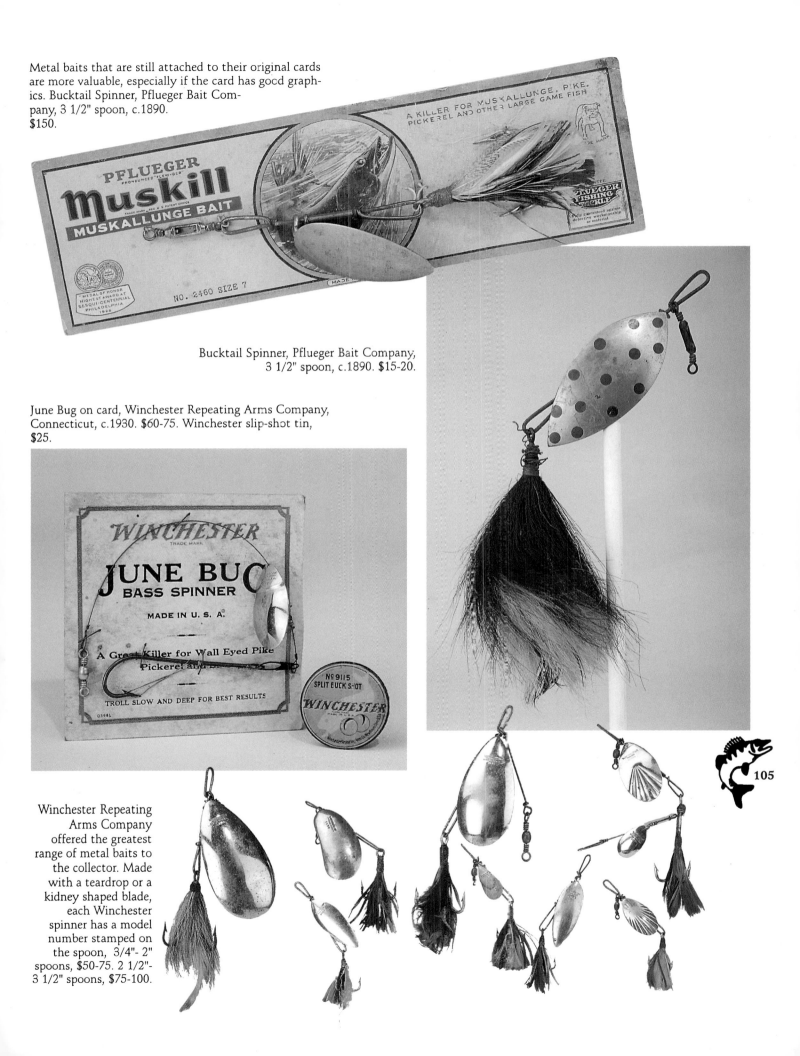

Bucktail Spinner, Pflueger Bait Company, 3 1/2" spoon, c.1890. $15-20.

June Bug on card, Winchester Repeating Arms Company, Connecticut, c.1930. $60-75. Winchester slip-shot tin, $25.

Winchester Repeating Arms Company offered the greatest range of metal baits to the collector. Made with a teardrop or a kidney shaped blade, each Winchester spinner has a model number stamped on the spoon, 3/4"- 2" spoons, $50-75. 2 1/2"- 3 1/2" spoons, $75-100.

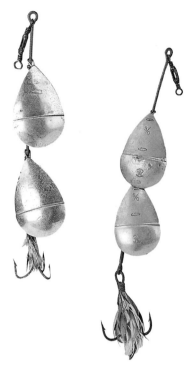

Unknown spinner bait, large spoon, 3 3/4", has a beaver logo stamp on the spoon leading collectors to believe this bait was produced by a Canadian company.

Lowe Double Musky Star Bait, W.T.J. Lowe, Buffalo, New York, c.1890. Although both of these lures have the same 3/0 (3 1/2") tear drop spoons, their rigging are different lengths. $25-30.

Full card of sunfish bobbers with attached line and hook, Carnival Cork Company, $25.

106

Folksy handmade baits can add an interesting slant to one's collection because they exhibited a wonderful flare for creativity, unknown maker, Minnesota, c.1930. $400-500 set.

Homemade spinner bait, northern Minnesota unknown maker, 4", spoon fashioned from brass DeLaval #15 cream separator label, c.1930. $10-15.

CHAPTER 4
THE AMERICAN REELS

The American multiplier reels developed by copying imported English fishing reels. Prior to the 1830s, few Americans had the time for sport angling, and those who did preferred English tackle. During this period of American history, the angler was forced to take his broken reels to a watchmaker, gunmaker, or blacksmith for repairs. So when American craftsmen began to manufacture reels, they started by copying English designs and technology which they adapted to the American style of angling. America's entry into the reel making market came in two areas of the country; in the North with a 2:1, and occasionally 3:1, multiplier called the New York reel, and in the South with a 4:1 ratio commonly known as the Blue Grass or Kentucky reel. George Synder (1781- 1841), Paris, Kentucky, changed the history of fishing by designing the first precision smooth-running multiplying reel that could be used for casting baits long distances. Before this, the reel was used primarily for storage of excess line. An angler would measure out as much line as he felt he needed to cast his bait and would hold the remaining line on his reel which was often a simple wooden spool.

Once the Americans entered the reel manufacturing business, several improvements were made to the reel. John C. Conroy, New York, considered to be the first professional American tacklemaker, introduced a balanced handle which maintained the spool's momentum, thereby allowing a greater casting distance and more evenly distributing wear on the ends of the spool shaft. The drag, which is one of the fundamental feature of modern day reels, was being built by American reelmakers Conroy and Jonathan F. and Benjamin F. Meek, Kentucky by the late 1840s, but there is no concrete evidence that these men were the inventors of this mechanism. American reelmakers fashioned reels with multi-gears that glided on garnet jewels with all the precision of their watchmaking skills. The first American reels were brass, quickly followed by German silver for the better quality reels. Hard rubber and nickel plating which were introduced to the reel making art in 1870 resulted in rare use of brass except under plating.

After the introduction of hard rubber and plating, German silver appeared only on the more expensive reels which were still hand-made individually. These reels are beautifully balanced and are considered an art — a collector doesn't have to understand the mechanics of the reel itself to appreciate it. Their rarity also makes them a good collectible. One must remember that a German silver multiplier reel cost about $35 at the same time a sportsman could buy a good rifle for $10.

By 1860, American reelmakers had established themselves as premier makers of multiplier reels but it wasn't until the 1870s that the demand for fly fishing tackle clamored for quality single action reels. C.F. Orvis, Vermont received a patent for his classic fly reel design in 1874. His reel was constructed of a narrow frame with pillar connected, perforated hard rubber headplates whose edges were strengthened by peripheral metal rings.

proved line drying and significantly lighted the reel without structurally weakening it. Orvis's concept of perforation was copied in one way or another by most other fly reel makers.

Prior to 1915 there were relatively few companies involved in reel making and as one would expect, these reels are rare. Trade reels which include private labels and house names of companies, that for whatever reason wanted to market a reel with their own brand name, are also considered highly collectible. Winchester Repeating Arms would be an excellent example of a trade reel. Reels that were mass produced are more common as one would expect, but many are still considered collectible.

William H. Talbot Reel Company, "Niangua", Nevada, c.1910. $600-800.

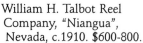

William H. Talbot Reel Company, "Vim" model manufactured for VL&A (Von Lengerke & Antoine Sporting Goods Store), Chicago, Illinois, c.1900. $800-1000.

William H. Talbot
Reel Company,
"Star" Model, Kansas
City, Missouri,
c.1910. $300-400.

William H. Talbot, "Ben-Hur", fly reel, c.1890. $2000-3000.

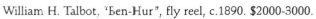

Benjamin C. Milam & Son, "Rustic" #3, Frankfort, Kentucky, c.1880. $400-500.

Benjamin F. Meek & Sons, "Blue Grass" #3, Louisville, Kentucky, c.1880. $400-450.

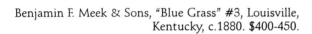

Benjamin F. Meek & Sons, "Meek" #33, nickel-plated brass reel, Louisville Kentucky, c.1900. $175-200.

Left to right: Peoria Casting Club Badge, owned by President William Shaffer, c.1940. $25-50; Benjamin F. Meek & Sons, "Meek" #3, Louisville, Kentucky, c.1890. $400-450; Horton Manufacturing, "Meek" #3, c.1930. $250-300.

Horton Manufacturing, "Meek" #7 with leather case, c.1920. $400-450.

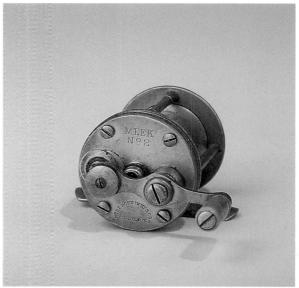

Horton Manufacturing, "Meek" #2, Bristol, Connecticut, c.1920. $400-500.

Horton Manufacturing, Bristol, "Blue Grass Simplex" #25 with leather carrying case, c.1920, $200-250.

111

Horton Manufacturing "Blue Grass Simplex" #25 with attached thumb guard, c.1920. $200-250.

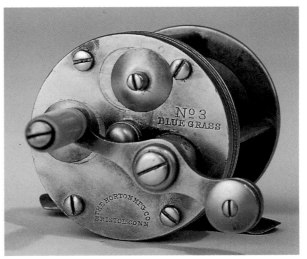

Horton Manufacturing, "Blue Grass" #25, c.1920. $150-200.

Horton Manufacturing. "Blue Grass" #3, c.1920. $300-400.

Horton Manufacturing. "Blue Grass" #4, c.1920. $300-400.

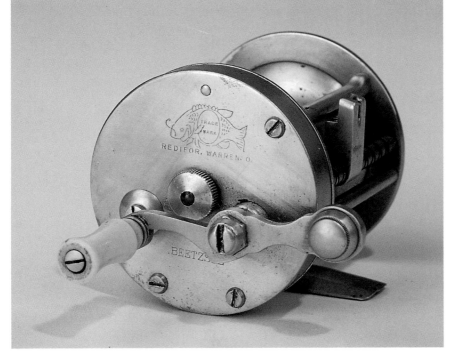

Redifor Rod & Reel Company, "Beetzsel" model, Warren, Ohio, c.1900. $300-400.

Carlton Manufactur-
ing Company, "4
Multiple", Rochester,
New York, c.1905.
$400-500.

Neptune Reel Company, " Neptune Special
Tournament Reel", c.1920. $100-150.

No. 4100   86 Yards

LEVEL WIND
FISHING REEL
QUADRUPLE MULTIPLYING

Bullard & Gormley Company, "Amacoy" #4100,
Chicago, Illinois, c.1910. $200-300.

113

American Ball Bearing Company, Rockford, Illinois. *Left:* "America" #1, c.1902. $400-500. *Right:* "America" #2, c.1902. $400-500.

Louisville Reel Works, "Louisville Casting Reel", Louisville, Kentucky, c.1920. $75-100.

Louisville Reel Works, "Model Casting Reel", c.1930. $100-125.

Julius Von Hofe, Brooklyn, New York, c.1920. *Left:* Fly reel. $200-300. *Right:* Bait casting reel, c.1920. $100-150.

Winchester Repeating Arms Company, trade reels, c.1920. *Left to right:* #2296, #2293, #2286. $100-150 each. Winchester tackle pocket catalog, c.1920 $25-35.

VL&A (Von Lengerke & Antoine Sporting Goods) "Professional", Chicago, Illinois, c.1920. $75-100.

115

VL&A, "Expert" #3 trade reel, probably produced by B.F. Meek & Son Company or Talbot Reel Company, c.1900. $300-400.

Pflueger Bait Company, "Buck-Eye". Akron, Ohio, c.1930. $175-200.

Left: Pflueger, "Supreme", with box, c.1940. $40-50. *Right:* Pflueger fish hooks in box. $10-15.

Pflueger Bait Company. *Left:* "Summit", with box, c.1930. $30-35. *Right:* "Supreme", with box, c.1940. $40-50.

Left to right:
Pflueger reel oil.
$5-10; Pflueger fish
hooks in box. $5-
10; Pflueger Bait
Company, #2800
reel, c.1960. $75-
100.

Pflueger Bait Company, "Redifor" Arkon,
Ohio, c.1920. $200-250.

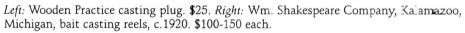

Left: Wooden Practice casting plug. $25. *Right:* Wm. Shakespeare Company, Kalamazoo,
Michigan, bait casting reels, c.1920. $100-150 each.

Wm. Shakespeare Company, "Marhoff" with box and reel oil, c.1950. $35-50.

Wm. Shakespeare Company fly reel with box, c.1950. $25-35. Shakespeare Company fishing line in box, $5-10.

South Bend Bait Company, fly reel #10 with box, c.1950. $35-40.

119

South Bend Bait Company, "Oreno-O-Matic" with box, c. 1940. $40-50.

James Heddon & Sons, Dowagiac, Michigan, bait casting reel #45, c.1920. $175-200.

James Heddon & Sons, bait casting reel #335, c.1920. $175-200.

Unknown maker, "Imbrie" Tournament reel, c.1920. $100-150.

A. B. Urfabiken, "Ambassodeur Record" #5000, c.1960. $50-75. If this reel has a pinhole in the handle cap it is worth $150-200.

Penn Fishing Tackle Manufacturing, Philadelphia, Pennsylvania, black rubber casting reel, c.1935. $40-50.

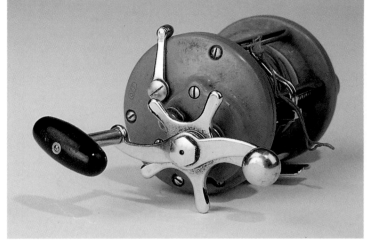

Penn Fishing Tackle Manufacturing, Green hard rubber casting reel, c.1950. $25-35.

Unknown maker, typical "Orvis" type fly reel, c.1930. $25-35.

CHAPTER 5
CREELS AND BAIT BOXES

A successful fisherman is often faced with a pleasant dilemma: what to do with his catch while he continues to fish? The answer--the fishing creel. North Woods Indians fashioned all sorts of containers out of birch bark including fishing creels. Laced with sinew or willow strips, birch bark creels, especially those decorated with berry-stain designs, are excellent examples of Native American craftsmanship and the rarest of the collectible fishing creels.

The emerging American sports angler found that the canvas creels and leather fish bags imported from Europe quickly became waterlogged and ungainly. When he was exposed to the fine basketry of the Native American, he realized basketry provided a perfect material for a portable container to hold his catch. Commonly used by trout fishermen who waded along creek beds, the basket creel was lightweight and allowed any excess water to run off so the creel was never cumbersome. The basket creel could be curved to fit a man's torso. A fish could be easily put through a hole either offset or centered in a securely hinged lid which guaranteed no lively fish would escape even if the fisherman lost his footing and fell into the water. Small creels were sometimes attached to a man's belt, but usually a harness was added to the creel to free the fisherman's hands.

Birch bark creel, Chippewa (Ojibwa), Wisconsin/ Canadian border, pine tree, rabbit and flying birds berry stained designs, leather ties and strap, 14"L x 10"H x 9"D, c.1930. $2000-2500.

123

Birch bark creel, Chippewa (Ojibwa), Wisconsin/Canadian border, pine tree, rabbit and flying birds berry stained designs, leather ties and strap, 14"L x 10"H x 9"D, c.1930. $2000-2500.

The earliest basketry creels were constructed out of wooden splints like market baskets. Splint are long narrow strips of wood; mostly ash, willow, or oak. Before commercial splint, which is machine cut into extremely thin veneer, splint was produced by the laborious process of soaking logs, splitting them and using a froe or drawknife to shave long individual strips of wood that were then sized by hand. Hand-cut splints are usually thicker, about an eighth of an inch thick, and irregularly shaped. The surface of hand-cut splint is rougher too because a splint cutting machine has a planing effect that smoothes the wood. Creels made of hand-cut splint as a rule predate 1880 when splint cutting machinery became readily available. To form the creel, splints were simply woven over and under splint or willow spokes. Better splint creels have twine or sweetgrass woven into decorative bands.

Willow basketry became popular when farmers from the Finger Lakes region of New York began to cultivate Purple and Caspian Willow for commercial use during the 1870s. By the 1880s manufacturers could run green willow through a machine that would produce uniformly shaped and sized caning material. Willow creels were now able to be produced commercially. Individual craftsmen found a ready market for their creels as did sporting goods distributors like L.L.Bean, Maine. There are as many different styles of willow creels as any other type of basketry.

Some weaving techniques combine splint and willow. The French weave creels are especially beautiful with a tight twining pattern formed with finely split willow. The twining technique twists multiple strands of split willow as they are passed over and under solid willow spokes creating a stronger finely woven basket.

Leather accents, added to creels to reinforce their construction, also increase their value to the collector. Leather harnesses are the most common adornment but extra leather pockets, pouches, and decorative bands were also added. Unusual latches are another feature that determines the collectibility of a creel. Wooden latches can be carved into little figures. Commercial makers often design a distinguishing latch. L.L. Bean's creel has a brass fish plate embossed unto their leather latch. A word of caution: willow creels are still being produced. Older creels take on a soft mellow patina. A coat of varnish stain is often added to a newer creels in attempt to fool a novice collector. Watch for darkening agents that tend to pool in the basket weave. An old creel will darken from use and the fish oils that penetrate the basketry. This natural darkening will be even inside and out though there may have rubbing at usage points. Old willow also has a smooth finish. Fine rough edges can sometimes be seen on the actual willow strands of a new basket.

"Turtle Trade Mark" creel, Michigan, full willow weave, wooden measure bar woven into lid, identifying wooden carved turtle latch stamped "TURTLE TRADE MARK", 14"L x 8"H x 6"D, c.1900. $1000-1500.

George Lawrence Company Creel #15, Portland, Oregon, split willow french weave, tooled leather reinforcements, strap, and 5" x 9" poach, creel measures 14"L x 10"H x 6"D, c.1920. $400-500.

Unknown maker, full willow creel, Minnesota, leather reinforcements, buckle, and straps, 14"L x 10"H x 6"D, c.1920. $300-400.

Unknown maker, full willow creel, Minnesota, handmade, wooden latch, braided rope loops for belt, 15"L x 10"H x 8"D, c.1930. $300-400.

The fisherman sometimes needed a container to hold his live bait. It was important to keep one's bait alive for this provided the best luring success. Various species of minnow were the most common type of live bait. Several companies produced minnow buckets which consisted of a perforated bucket that fit inside another solid bucket that was often imprinted with interesting graphics. Bass fishermen also found crickets, grasshoppers, and other larger bugs made good bait. Insects were carried in wire mesh boxes.

Cricket boxes that were painted and decorated are very collectible. Anytime extra care was taken to embellish one's fishing equipment the value of that item increases. Take for example this simple wooden tackle box that was presented to Jimmy Robinson. Robinson was the staff outdoor writer for the *Minneapolis Star Tribune*, a staff writer with *Sports Afield Magazine*, and author of several sporting books. This providence and the quality of the craftsmanship evident in the tackle box itself creates a collectible.

Old Pal Company, Pennsylvania, "Old Pal" Minnow bucket, c.1930. $100-150.

Anchor Company, "Kingfisher" minnow bucket, c.1940. $200-300.

126

Old Pal/Woodstream Company, Pennsylvania, Old Pal Minnow bucket, c.1960. $75-100.

Live bait box, unknown maker, Minnesota, homemade, wooden and wire mesh, wire handle, c.1930. $75-100.

 127

Live bait box, Morley Johnson, Palisade, Minnesota, handmade, painted, c.1920. $300-400.

One-of-a-kind tackle box presented to Jimmy Robinson, noted outdoors writer known to many as "Mr. Minnesota", cedar with brass hardware, c.1940. $400-500.

Top view of personalized tackle box presented to Jimmy Robinson.

128

Jimmy's wife, Clara, who helped run his hunting and fishing camp in Canada is characterized with Jimmy in his fishing boat.

Inscriptions referring to Robinson's reputation as a social drinker and his association with *Sports Afield* suggest this tackle box was probably presented at a roast for Robinson.

Another useful piece of equipment for the fisherman was his landing net. While today's landing nets are formed from hollow aluminum tubing and nylon netting, early landing nets were usually made of wooden and cotton net. Sturdy ash or cedar was steamed and bent to form a loop to hold the netting. The handle was wrapped with leather or split willow caning. Some landing nets were made to fold so they could be carried out of the way on one's belt as the fisherman waded through the water casting for fish. Identifying markings and quality workmanship determine the value of a landing net.

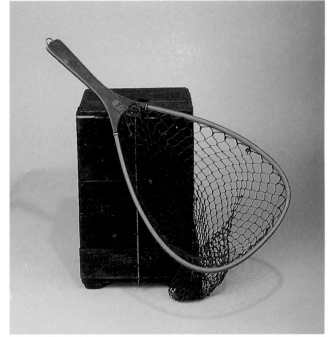

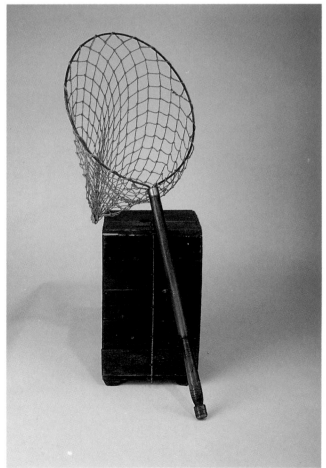

Above:
Folding landing net, brass fitting, cotton netting, bent wood with cane wrappings, c.1990. $200-250.

Top right photo:
Landing net, unknown maker, bent wood with cotton netting, c.1920. $75-100.

Right:
Landing net, George Herter's Incorporated, Waseca, Minnesota, cedar handle, wire loop and cotton netting, c.1950. $50-75.

Chapter 6
Fish Models and Plaques

The practice of carving replica fish for the wall became popular after fly fishing became an aristocratic past time in the court of George IV of England (1820-1830). The art of taxidermy had not developed well enough to "put up" the trophy fish successfully for any length of time and the alternative plaster of Paris castings were heavy and ungainly. Life-sized wooden fish models probably evolved from the practice of tracing a fish's outline on a board for a permanent record. Fish model makers were active through out the salmon and trout fishing areas of England, Norway, and Scotland.

As part of the English Empire, European-style fish models were also found in Canada. It was in the New England states, especially Maine, where the American art of carving fish models became prevalent. George Gillet of Rhode Island, an English immigrant and retired taxidermist (c.1910), is accredited with being the first professional American fish model maker. While European-style fish models were created following the tradition of capturing trophy fish by duplicating the actual measurements of the fish, American professional artisans and regional folk artists started creating a new type of fish plaque which was carved strictly as an ornamental piece.

In the Midwest fish plaques developed into a strong folk art form. Local craftsmen created fanciful replicas of the native fish; perch, trout, sunfish, crappies, bass, pickerel, and northern pike. While most carvers tried to emulate life-like fish, others like Oscar Peterson, Cadillac, Michigan carved highly stylish fish plaques. Fish carvings were sometimes mounted on painted scenes and decorated boards. Fish plaques were sold at local taverns and sporting goods stores through Minnesota, Michigan, and Wisconsin to local sportsmen and visiting tourists. These fish plaques are just recently being recognized as a viable folk art form.

Fish model European style, James Crawford, Maine, 4# 14 ounce pickerel, 26 1/2" in original gold gild frame, c.1900. $4000-5000.

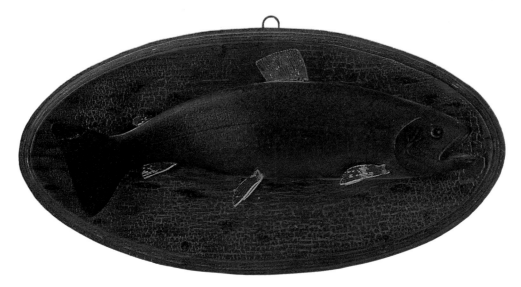

Fish model European style, brown trout, 11", signed
"Reginald O. Edwards, McFalls (Mechanics Falls), Maine,"
c.1930. $2000-2500.

Fish model European style, jumping brown trout, 11",
Reginald O. Edwards, Mechanics Falls, Maine, c.1930.
$2000-2500. *Photo by Gene Kangas. Courtesy of Gene and
Linda Kangas.*

Fish model European style, eastern brook trout, 23",
caught on Rangley Lake c.1949. Carved by Phillippe Sirois
(1893-1980), Bath, Maine, it is the largest known trout
carving by Sirois. $3000-4000.   *Photo by Gene Kangas.
Courtesy of Gene and Linda Kangas.*

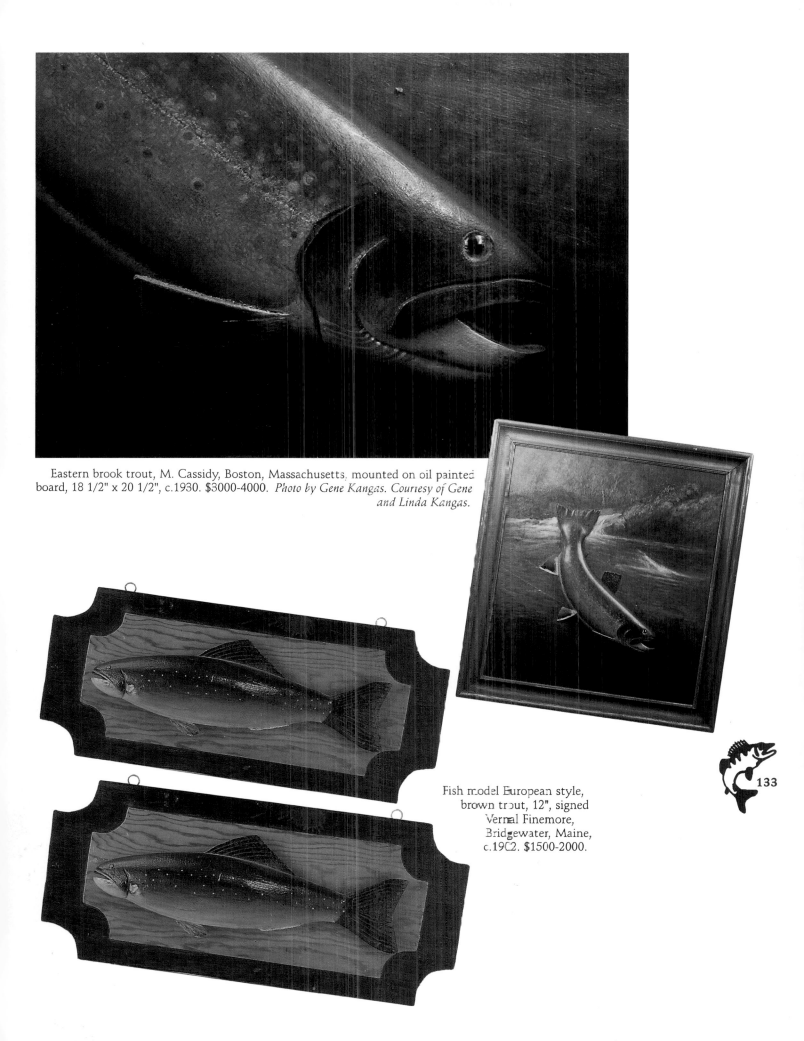

Eastern brook trout, M. Cassidy, Boston, Massachusetts, mounted on oil painted board, 18 1/2" x 20 1/2", c.1930. $3000-4000. *Photo by Gene Kangas. Courtesy of Gene and Linda Kangas.*

Fish model European style, brown trout, 12", signed Vernal Finemore, Bridgewater, Maine, c.1902. $1500-2000.

133

Although Fred Lexow was possibly the most prolific of the Minnesota fish plaque makers, he created less than fifty fish plaques. Made strictly as cabin decorations, his trout carvings were mounted on boards which he often wood-grained and embellished with painted aquatic plants. Lexow trout are fat 3/4 round body carvings.

Only known double fish plaque by Fred Lexow made for Bitner's Resort, Balsam Lake, Minnesota, c.1930. *Left:* brook trout with metal tail and fins, 13 1/2". *Right:* Rainbow trout with wooden tail and fins, 13". $5000-6000.

Rainbow trout, wooden tail and metal fins with open mouth, 14", c.1935. $3000-3500.

134

Brook trout, wooden tail and metal fins, open mouth, 14 1/2", c.1940. $2500-3000.

Brook trout, wooden tail and fins, 14",
c.1925. $3000-3500.

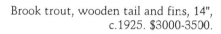

This mirror image set of 1/2 sized trout (9 1/2")
was carved for John Plank, Balsam Lake, a
neighbor and close friend of Lexow, c.1935.
$1500 each

Brown trout, earliest known fish plaque by Raymond Thompson, Park Rapids. c.1920. His later work evolved into exceptionally realistic carvings. $750-1000.

Jumping large mouth bass attributed to John Tax, Osakis, Minnesota, who is better known for his smaller fish plaques made for tourist trade and decoys.

Trout, 14", by Louis Labotta (1889-1993), contemporary and student of wildlife artist Owen Gromne, New Lisbon, Wisconsin, c.1940. $2500-3000.

Brown trout, 16", by Louis Labotta, c.1940. $2500-3000.

137

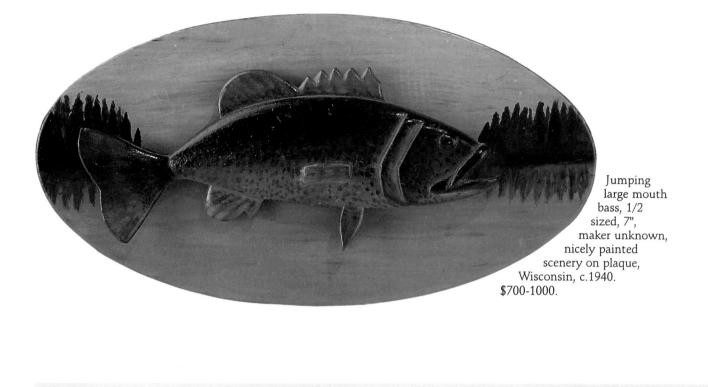

Jumping
large mouth
bass, 1/2
sized, 7",
maker unknown,
nicely painted
scenery on plaque,
Wisconsin, c.1940.
$700-1000.

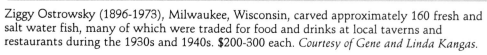

Ziggy Ostrowsky (1896-1973), Milwaukee, Wisconsin, carved approximately 160 fresh and salt water fish, many of which were traded for food and drinks at local taverns and restaurants during the 1930s and 1940s. $200-300 each. *Courtesy of Gene and Linda Kangas.*

Northern pike, maker unknown, 44", c.1940. $500-750.

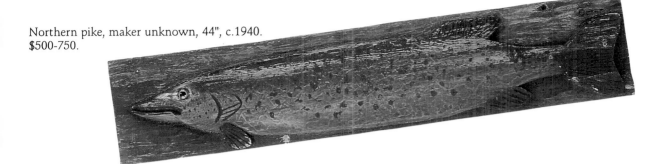

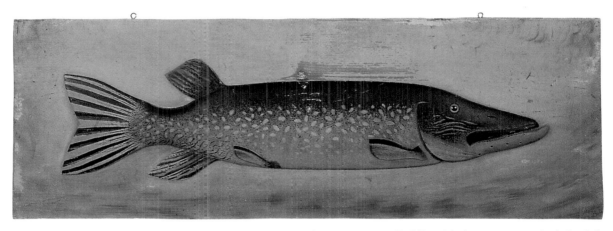

Oscar Peterson, Cadillac, Michigan, approached the fish model in a unique manner. He carved out the fish image in relief creating a one-piece plaque. Northern pike, 26" X 11", c.1930. $5000-7000. *Photo by Alan Haid. Courtesy of David Fisher.*

Peterson often signed his plaques by nailing a copper fur trapping tag to the outer edge of the plaque. *Photo by Alan Haid. Courtesy of David Fisher.*

John Williams, New Boston, Illinois, fish plaque, northern pike. 40". c.1950. $1000-1200;
John Williams, turtle, 16", c.1950. $300-500.

140

Edward Forman, Antioch, Illinois, fish plaque, signed, Black crappie, 10", c.1943.
$1500-2000.

CHAPTER 7
TRADE SIGNS AND MISCELLANEOUS FOLK ART

Another interesting field of collecting fishing paraphernalia is based on the need to advertise. Aside from printed advertising like pamphlets, calendars, and other types of paper products which could fill another book on their own, there was a variety of three dimensional art created by commercial and folk artists. Most tackle stores had some kind of tackle sign that would be visible from the road. Once inside a shop, large reproductions of lure, fish decoys, and other related models often beckoned to prospective customers. Any given dirt road in the northern midwest states is dotted with delightful cabin signs that capture the personalities of the their owners. Small resorts often relied solely upon word-of-mouth and charming roadside signs to get visiting tourists to stop. National outdoors magazines and larger tackle companies kept wildlife artists busy creating cover art for their publications. It is a shame that present day graphics are not as interesting and colorful. Although size prevents most collectors from owning more than a few of these great accenting pieces, they are worthy of recognition.

Northern pike, by Oscar Peterson, Cadillac, Michigan, one of three known large (4'-5') trade fish, wood with metal fins, 48", c.1925. $15000-20000. *Photo by Alan Haid. Collection of Alan and Elaine Haid.*

Northern pike, wood with metal fins, only known smaller trade sign, 27", c.1925. $7000-9000. *Photo by Alan Haid. Collection of Alan and Elaine Haid.*

Trade Sign, jumping northern pike, hung in entrance alcove of Eveleth, Minnesota hardware store, 48", c.1920. $750-1000.

Trade sign, Northern pike, Northern Minnesota, 41", c.1940. $300-400.

142

Bait sign, sunfish, 20", c.1940. $150-200.

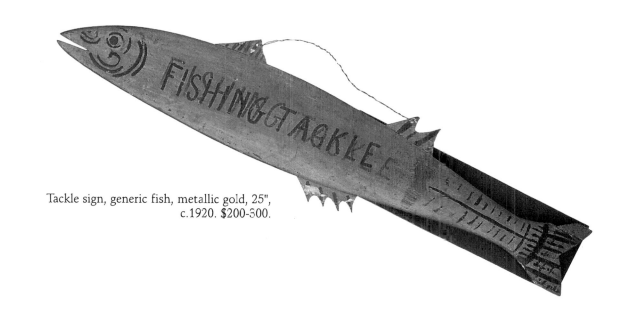

Tackle sign, generic fish, metallic gold, 25",
c.1920. $200-300.

Porcelain
sign, "Fishing licenses sold", double-
sided, 10" x 26", Wisconsin, c.1935. $200-300.

Fish refuge sign, porcelain, 13" X 18", c.1940. $200-300.

Ted Bailey, Princeton, Illinois, enjoying fishing on Gull Lake, Brainerd, Minnesota where he and a group of friends had a cabin. *Photos courtesy of Mrs. Ted Bailey.*

Cabin sign, wooden fish with names of Ted Bailey and other members of Princeton Game & Fish Club, Princeton, Illinois who shared a cabin on Gull Lake, Brainerd Minnesota, 26", c.1940. $50-75.

Camp sign, primitive wooden, Minnesota,
16" X 24", c.1920. $200-300.

Cabin sign, plaster of paris fish, oil on board painting,
Butternut, Wisconsin, c.1920. $400-500.

Trade sign, porcelain, double-sided, Evinrude
Motors Dealer, c.1915. $1000-1200.

Trade coaster, tin, Evinrude Motors, c.1920. $300-400.

Store display, rainbow trout, wooden with cardboard fins and tail, c.1930. $300-400.

Store display, Bass-Oreno style plug, handmade, unknown maker, Minnesota, 48", c.1935. $400-500.

Store Display, Shakespeare mouse style plug, handmade, unknown maker, Minnesota, 6 1/2", c.1935. $150-200.

Store Display, Bass-Oreno style plug, handmade, unknown maker, Minnesota, 6 1/2", c.1925. $150-200.

Cover art, oil on board, 8" x 10", unsigned, c.1935. $150-200.

Cover art, stretched canvas, 16" x 20", unsigned, c.1920. $300-400.

149

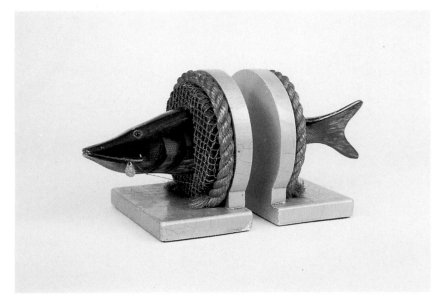

Folk art bookends, R E. Warren, Cedarville, Massachusetts, carved and painted wood, glass eyes, metal lure in mouth, and rope, 12"L X 6 1/4"H X 6"W, c.1940. $500-750. *Photo by Gene Kangas. Courtesy of Gene and Linda Kangas.*

Folk art weather vane, blue fish, Ivan Amist, Grand Rapids, Minnesota, 42", c.1940. $800-1000.

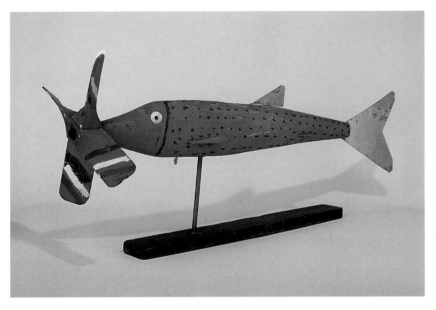

Folk art weather vane, double vane, maker unknown, Minnesota, fisherman in boat 22"L x 17"H x 5"D, and northern pike 28"L x 7"H x 4"D, c.1930. $2000-3000.

Fishing Contest poster, Given Hardware, Bemidji, Minnesota, 11" x 14", c.1938. $50-75.

A group of sportsmen proudly display braces of birds and double stringers of panfish. Original photograph c.1900. $50-75.

Douglas Moseley, Princeton, Illinois displays a trophy northern catch on Black Duck Lake, Minnesota, c.1890. *Photo courtesy of Frances McGonigle.*

151

Fisherman ready to hit the road to northern Minnesota, c.1925. *Photo courtesy of Mrs. Ted Bailey.*

RESOURCES

BOOKS

Alexander Henry's Travels & Adventures in the Years 1760-1776. Edited by Milo Milton Quaife, Chicago, Lakeside Press, 1921.

The American Sporting Collector's Handbook. Edited by Allan J. Liu. Tulsa, Winchester Press, 1982.

Baron, Frank R., Carver, Raymond L. Bud Stewart, *Michigan's Legendary Lure Maker*. Hillsdale, Ferguson, 1990

Baron, Frank R. *One fish, Two Fish, Green Fish, Blue Fish*. Livonia, Baron Inc.

Calabi, Silvo. *Antique Fishing Tackle*. Secaucus, The Welfleet Press, 1989.

Harrell, Loy S. *Decoys of Lake Champlain*. West Chester, Schiffer Publishing Ltd., 1986.

Kangas, Gene and Linda. *Decoys*. Paducah, Collector Books, 1992.

Kimball, Art, Brad & Scott. *The Fish Decoy: Volume I*. Boulder Junction, Aardark Publications, Incorporated, 1986.

___. *The Fish Decoy: Volume II*. Boulder Junction, Aardark Publications, Incorporated, 1987.

___. *The Fish Decoy: Volume III*. Boulder Junction, Aardark Publications, Incorporated, 1993.

___. *Early Fishing Lures of America*. Boulder Junction, Aardark Publications, Incorporated, 1985.

Kimball, Art & Scott. *Collecting Old Fishing Tackle*. Boulder Junction, Aardark Publications, Incorprated, 1980.

Kinietz, W. Vernon. *Indians of the Western Great Lakes--1615-1760*. Ann Arbor, University of Michigan Press, 1965.

Kohl, Johana. *Kitaki Gami (Wanderings Round Lake Superior)*. London. Chapman & Hall.

Luckey Carl F. *Old Fishing Lures and Tackle*. Florence, Books Americana, 1993.

Murphy, Dudley and Edmiston, Rick. *Fishing Lure Collectibles*. Paducah, Collector Books, 1995.

Munger, Albert J. *Those Old fishing Reels*. Philadelphia, Albert J. Munger, 1982.

Petersen, Donald J. *Folk Art Fish Decoys*. Atglen, Schiffer Publishing Ltd., 1996.

Saliva, Marcel L. *Ice Fishing Spears*. Potomac, MarJac Publications, 1993.

Swanson, Ronald S., *Fish Model: An Exhibition*. Manchester, American Museum of Fly Fishing, 1992-1993.

Vernon, Steve K. *Antique Fishing Reels*. Harrisburg, Stackpole Books, 1985.

Vernon, Steve K. and Stewart, Frank M., III. *Fishing Reel Makers of Kentucky*. Plano, Thomas B Reel Co., 1992.

White, Karl T. *Fishing Tackle Antiques*. Arcadia. Karl T. White, 1987.

The National Lure Collectors Club Magazine, Springfield, Missouri, Dudley Murphy, editor.

ARTICLES

Dickert, Harold. "Autobiography of Gordon Saltonstall Hubbard, 1863", *National Fishing Lure Collectors' Club Gazette*, vol. 20, #30, Spring/March, 1986.

Esary, Daune. "The Ancient Art of Decoy Fishing", *The Living Museum*, vol. 55, #1, 1993.

Guthrie, Greg. "John Snow", *Decoy Magazine*, January/February 1996.

Kangas, Gene and Linda. "Lake Chautaugua-Spear Fishing", *Decoy Magazine*, September/October, 1988.

Kimball, Art & Scott. "Native American Spearfishing Decoys of The Upper Midwestern Great Lakes States", *Decoy Magazine*, November/December, 1995.

Swanson, Ronald S. "Fish Models, Plaques, and Effigies", *Decoy Magazine*, July/August, 1996.

PUBLICATIONS BY DONNA TONELLI

"Fred Lexow, Minnesota Folk Artist". *Decoy Magazine*, July/August, 1989.

"Leroy Howell". *Decoy Magazine*, Nov/Dec, 1990.

"Ernest Newman-Minnesota Master Tackle Maker", *Decoy Magazine*, March/April, 1991.

"John Albert Ryden--Fish Maker from Aitkin County", *Decoy Magazine*, May/June, 1991.

"Frank Mizera-Minnesota Fish Decoy Maker", *Decoy Magazine*, July/August 1991.

"William 'Slow' Batters: Minnesota's Real 'Harry Blancherd'", *Decoy Magazine*, Sept/Oct, 1991.

"Bethel Decoys: Continuing a Family Tradition", *Decoy Magazine*, Jan/Feb,1992.

"John Tax: A Minnesota Whittler", *Decoy Magazine*, March/April, 1992.

"Interest in Fish Decoys Grows by Leaps and Bounds", *Decoy Magazine*, May/June, 1992.

"Chester 'Chet' Sawyer, True Folk Artist of the North Woods", *Decoy Magazine*, July/August 1992.

"Ray Thompson, Maker of Superb Fishing Tackle and Fish Decoys", *Decoy Magazine*, Sept/Oct, 1992.

"Chuck Hall, Carving Out the Good Life", *Decoy Magazine*, Jan/Feb, 1993.

"Copper Fish Decoys, Casting Variety and Form", *Decoy Magazine*, Nov/Dec, 1993.

"Heddon & Sons Inc., Breaking the Ice with Spearing Decoys", *Decoy Magazine*, Jan/Feb, 1994.

"Tackle Companies Market to Hearty Spear Fishermen", *Decoy Magazine*, May/June, 1994.

"LaCrosse River Spear Fishing Decoys", *Decoy Magazine*, March/April 1995.

"The Lure of Frogs", *Decoy Magazine*, July/August 1995.

COLLECTING ORGANIZATIONS

American Fish Decoy Association
    (newsletter)
c/o John Shoffner
624 Merritt
Fife Lake, Michigan 49633

Great Lakes Fish Decoy Collectors & Carvers Association (newsletter)
c/o Frank R. Baron
35824 W. Chicago
Livonia, Michigan 48150

National Fishing Lure Collectors Club
(quarterly magazine)
P.O. Box 13
Grove City, Ohio 43123

Midwest Decoy Collectors Association
(sporting collectibles)
c/o Herb Desch
3006 Fox Glen Court
St. Charles, Illinois 60174

153

For more information, write:
Donna Tonelli
P.O. Box 459
Lake Andes, SD 57356
Phone: 605-337-2301

TACKLE MANUFACTURERS

A

Abbey & Imbrie
New York, New York

Abercrombie & Fitch Co.
New York, New York

Action Lure Co.
Hollywood, California

Adolf Arntz
Muskegon, Michigan

W. & J.M. Aikenhead
Rochester, New York

Franklin Alger
Grand Rapids, Michigan

Allstar Bait Co.
Chicago, Illinois

154

Forrest Allen
Stanford, Connecticut

Alliance Mfg., Co.
Alliance, Ohio

American Display Co.
Akron, Ohio

Angler's Supply Co.
Utica, New York

Fred Arbogast Co., Inc.
Akron, Ohio

T.F. Auclair & Assoc., Inc.
Detroit, Michigan

B

Barr-Royer Co.
Waterloo, Iowa

Bass-King
Brushton, New York

Bear Creek Bait Co.
Kaleva, Michigan

Becker Sheward Mfg., Co.
Council Bluffs, Iowa

Benson-Vaile Co.
Kokomo, Indiana

Berry-Lebeck Mfg. Co.
California, Missouri

Biek Mfg. Co.
Dowagiac, Michigan

Biff Bait Co.
Milwaukee, Wisconsin

A.F. Bingenheimer
Milwaukee, Wisconsin

Bite-Em Bait Co.
Fort Wayne. Indiana

Bleeding Bait Mfg. Co.
Dallas, Texas

Bomber Bait Co.
Gainesville, Texas

T.J. Boulton
Detroit; Michigan

Bright-Eye Lure Products
Detroit, Michigan

Broadcaster Lures
Youngstown. Ohio

Brook Shiner Bait Co.
Milwaukee, Wisconsin

H. Corbin Brush
Brushton, New York

Julio Buel
Whitehall, New York

Paul Bunyan Bait Co.
Minneapolis, Minnesota

Burke Bait Co.
Chicago, Illinois

C

Carter's Bestever Bait Co.
Indianapolis, Indiana

Charmer Minnow Co.
Springfield, Missouri

Chicago Tackle Co.
Chicago, Illinois

Thomas Chubb
Post Mills, Vermont

Cisco Kid Tackle, Inc.
Boca Raton, Florida

C.A. Clark Co.
Springfield Missouri

Harry Comstock
Fulton, New York

Max Cook
Denver Colorado

Dave Cook Sporting Goods
Denver, Colorado

Crall Brothers
Chicago Junction, Ohio

Creek Chub Bait Co.
Garret, Indiana

D

Dame, Stoddard & Kendall
Boston, Mass.

Decker Bait Co.
Brooklyn, New York

Detroit Bait Co.
Detroit, Michigan

Detroit Glass Minnow Tube
Co.
Detroit, Michigan

Detroit Weedless Bait Co.
Detroit, Michigan

Diamond Mfg. Co.
St Louis, Missouri

Dickens Bait Co.
Fort Wayne, Indiana

James L. Donaly
Bloomfield New Jersey

Harry Drake
Milwaukee, Wisconsin

Druly Research Products
Prescott, Wisconsin

E

Eagle Claw (Wright & McGill)
Denver, Colorado

Eckfield Boat Co.
Algonac, Michigan

Eger Bait Mfg. Co.
Bartow, Florida

Electric Luminous Submarine
Bait Co.
Milwaukee, Wisconsin

R.S. Elliot Arms Co.
Kansas City, Missouri

Enterprise Mfg. Co.
Akron, Ohio

Lou Eppinger Mfg. Co.
Detroit, Michigan

Etchen Tackle Co.
Detroit, Michigan

Eureka Bait Co.
Coldwater, Michigan

F

Fenner Weedless Bait Co.
Oxford, Wisconsin

Fischer-Schuberth Co.
Chicago, Illinois

Fishathon Bait Mfg. Co., Inc.
Okmulgee, Oklahoma and
Ypsilanti, Michigan

Florida Fishing Tackle Co.
St Petersburg, Florida

Al Foss
Cleveland, Ohio

C.J. Frost
Stevens point, Wisconsin

H.J. Frost & Co.
New York, New York

G

George Gayle & Son
Frankfort, Kentucky

Gen-shaw
Kankakee, Illinois

Gladding Corporation
(South Bend)
Syracuse, New York

Goodwin Granger & Co.
Denver, Colorado

Grand Lake Fishing Tackle
Springfield, Missouri

J.F. Gregory
St. Louis, Missouri

H

Hastings Sporting Goods
Hastings, Michigan

W.B. Haynes
Akron, Ohio

James Heddon & Sons
Dowagiac, Michigan

Helin Tackle
Detroit, Michigan

Hibbard, Spencer, Bartlett &
Co.
Chicago, Illinois

Joe Hinkle
Louisville, Kentucky

J.C. Holzwarth
(Spring, Holzwarth & Co.)
Alliance, Ohio

155

Hom-art Bait Co.
Akron, Ohio

Hookzem Bait Co.
Chicago, Illinois

I

Immell Bait Co.
(Chippewa Bait)
Blair, Wisconsin

Isle Royale Bait Co.
Jackson, Michigan

J

W.J. Jamison
Chicago, Illinois

Louis Johnson Co.
Chicago, Illinois and
Highland Park, Illinois

Joy Bait Co.
Lansing, Michigan

K

Kalamazoo Fishing Tackle Mfg.
Kalamazoo, Michigan

Fred Keeling & Co.
Rockford, Illinois

H.H. Kiffe Co.
New York, New York

King Bait Co.
Minneapolis, Minnesota

K & K Mfg. Co.
Toledo, Ohio

A. Kleinman
New York, New York

Arthur J. Kumm
Dearborn, Michigan

L

L & S Bait Co.
Bradley, Illinois

Lazy Dazy Bait Co.
Preston, Minnesota

E.J. Lockhart Co.
Galesburg, Michigan

W.T.J. Lowe
Buffalo, New York

M

Makinew Tackle Co.
Kaleva, Michigan

McCormic Bait Co.
Kalamazoo, Michigan and
Warsaw, Indiana

Mepps (Sheldon's Inc.)
Antigo, Wisconsin

Mermade Bait Co., Inc.
Platteville, Wisconsin

Wm. Mills & Son
New York, New York
and Central Valley, New York

Millsite Fishing Tackle
Howell, Michigan

Moonlight Bait Co.
PawPaw, Michigan

H.C. Moore
Ypsilanti, Michigan

Myers & Spellman
Shelby, Michigan

N

Naturalure Bait Co.
Pasadena, California

New York Sporting Goods Co.
New York, New York

O

Orchard Industries
Detroit, Michigan

Outing Mfg. Co.
ELkhart, Indiana

Ozark Lure Co.
Tulsa, Oklahoma

P

F. A. Pardee & Co.
Kent, Ohio

PawPaw Bait Co.
PawPaw, Michigan

Payne Bait Co.
Chicago, Illinois

Joe E. Pepper
Rome, New York

Jim Pfeffer
Orlando, Florida

Pfeiffer Live Bait Holder Co.
Detroit, Michigan

Pflueger Sporting Goods
Columbus, South Carolina

Pico Lures
San Antonio, Texas

P & K
Momence, Illinois

Pontiac Mfg. Co.
Pontiac, Michigan

R

R.K. Tackle Co.
Grand Rapids, Michigan

Rawlings Sporting Goods, Co.
St. Louis, Missouri

Louis Rhead Nature Lures
Brooklyn and Amityville, New
York

Fred Rhodes
Kalamazoo, Michigan

Rider Casting Reel Co.
Fort Wayne, Indiana

Rod & Creel Tackle Co.
Detroit, Michigan

J.K. Rush
Syracuse, New York

S

Shakespeare Co.
Columbus, South Carolina

Shannon
Philadelphia, Pennsylvania

Shapleigh Hardware Co.
St. Louis, Missouri

Shoff Fishing Tackle Co.
Kent, Washington

Shure-bite Inc.
Bronson, Michigan

Silver Creek Novelty Co.
Dowagiac, Michigan

Simmons hardware Co.
St. Louis, Missouri

T.S. Skilton Mfg.
Winstead, Connecticut

G.M. Skinner
Clayton, new York

Jack K. Smithwick
Shreveport, Louisiana

South Bend Tackle Co.
(Gladding)
Syracuse, New York

Springfield Novelty Mfg. Co.
Springfield, Missouri

Charles Stapf
Prescott, Wisconsin

Bud Steward Tackle
Flint, Michigan

T

Toledo Bait Co.
Toledo, Ohio

Trappers Supply Co.
Oak Park, Illinois

True Temper
(American Fork & Hoe)
Geneva, Ohio

Tulsa Tackle Co.
Tulsa, Oklahoma

O.A. Turner
Coldwater, Michigan

O.C. Tuttle
Old Forge, New York

U

Union Springs Specialty Co.
Cayuga, New York

V

Vacuum Bait Co.
North Manchester, Indiana

Vaughn's Tackle Co.
Cheboygan, Michigan

Vex Bait Co.
Dayton, Ohio

Von Lengerke & Detmold Inc.
New York, New York

W

W.C. Mfg. Co.
Racine, Wisconsin

Weber Tackle Co.
(Weber Lifelike Fly Co.)
Stevens Point, Wisconsin

Edwin Weller Co.
Sioux City, Iowa

Weezel bait Co.
Cincinnati, Ohio

Wiggle Tail Minnow Co.
Detroit, Michigan

Wilkinson Co.
Chicago, Illinois

L.A. Wilford & Son
Jackson, Michigan

Wilmarth Tackle Co.
Roosevelt, New York

Thomas E. Wilson & Co.
(Wilson-Wester W. Sporting
   Goods Co.)
New York, Chicago, San Fran-
cisco

Clinton Wilt Mfg. Co.
Springfield, Missouri

Winchester Arms Co.
New Haven, Connecticut

Albert Winnie
Traverse City, Michigan

F.C. Woods & Co.
Alliance, Ohio

Wright and McGill
(Eagle Claw)
Denver, Colorado

Y

Yakima Bait Co.
Granger, Washington

Yawman & Erbe
Rochester, New York

Z

Zink Artificial Bait Co.
Dixon, Illinois

157

INDEX

159